HOUSEHOLD CONVENIENCES

And How to Make Them

THE LYONS PRESS

GUILFORD, CONNECTICUT
AN IMPRINT OF THE GLOBE PEQUOT PRESS

ALL RIGHTS RESERVED. No part of this book may be reproduced or transmitted in any form by any means, electronic or mechanical, including photocopying and recording, or by any information storage and retrieval system, except as may be expressly permitted by the 1976 Copyright Act or in writing from the publisher. Requests for permission should be addressed to The Lyons Press, P.O. Box 480, Guilford, CT 06437.

The Lyons Press is an imprint of the Globe Pequot Press.

Originally published in 1884 by Orange Judd Company

First Lyons Press edition, September 2001

Printed in Canada

2 4 6 8 10 9 7 5 3 1

The Library of Congress Cataloging-in-Publication Data is available on file.

ISBN 1-58574-374-7

INTRODUCTION.

———•◦•———

The Census of 1880 shows eight million nine hundred and fifty-five thousand eight hundred and twelve (8,955,-812) dwellings in the United States, in which nearly ten million families (9,945,916) live. During the past three years this number has been largely increased, so that we now have perhaps ten million dwellings, in our many cities, towns, villages, and scattered throughout the country.

A furnished house is not always a home. Carpets and furniture may be of the latest styles and costly, and yet the rooms fail to be home-like. It is only when a house has been occupied long enough to have an individuality imparted to it by its occupants, when a vast number of little articles, suggested by the daily wants of the family, have been made—they can not be bought—that the rooms have the aspect of home.

The present work brings together the devices that hundreds of house-keepers have found useful in their own homes, and they are offered in the hope that they will be welcome in the homes of many others. The "Conveniences" are selected on account of their practical character, trusting that they may lighten the labor and "save steps" to many an over-worked house-keeper.

(3)

In making the selection we have not been confined to the interior of the dwelling only.

The first impression of a house is received from its exterior, and it is not difficult to make that home-like, and indicative of the character of those who occupy it.

In the majority of houses—especially farm houses—the kitchen is the most· important room of all. Not only are the meals prepared here, but it is often used as a work-room in which to carry on various operations belonging to the farm. It is in the kitchen especially that conveniences are most needed, and special attention has been given to this division of the household, and its important adjuncts, the pantries and cupboards.

CONTENTS.

CHAPTER I.—AROUND THE HOUSE.

Foot Scrapers, or Boot Cleaners. How a Scraper was Made. A Portable Scraper and Mat. A Mud Mat. A Filter for a Cistern. Rain-Water Strainer. The Wastes of Country Houses. Make your own Hammock. A Home-Made Tent. A Shaded Garden Seat. Window Screens and Awnings. A Clothes-Line Reel. A Clothes-Line Holder. A Clothes-Line Elevator. A Revolving Clothes-Line. A Side-Shelf for Draining Bottles. A Folding Table for a Porch. Simple Ash Sifters. A Safe Ash-Bin. A Water Guard to a Window Brush. Wood-Rack and Wood-Apron. The Home Crematory. An Easily-Made Snow-Plow. Leaches, Lye and Soap. A Screen for the House. A Carriage Step. A Work-Stand for the Lawn. Vines at the Door. A Seat in the Grove. Where to Place Fly-Screens. Cistern Cheaply Made. A Fruit-Drying Arrangement. Drying Fruit under Sashes.... ....

CHAPTER II.—THE CELLAR.

Cellars in General. Musty Cellars. Ventilating a Cellar. Ice Boxes or Refrigerators. Preserving Small Quantities of Ice. A Meat Safe. Filter for Water. Conveniences for Weighing Small Articles. Cover to a Pork Barrel. A Milk Cupboard. A Home-Made Cheese Press. Butter Molds and Stamps. Convenient Cellar Window—Cool Room. Coal Bins. A Small Coal Box...

CHAPTER III.—THE KITCHEN.

Improve the Kitchen. A Flour Box. Box for Holding Spices. A Folding Ironing Table. A Convenient Side Table. Box for Holding Scouring Material. A Bread or Kneading Board. A Convenient Baking-Table. A Convenient Wash-Bench. An Improved Wash-Bench. Easy Washing of Clothes. Dish Sink with Racks for Draining. Vegetable Slicer and Grater. A Cabbage Cutter. A Home-Made Butter Worker. A Cooking Steam Pipe. Don't Spoil the Meats. Clothes Driers. A Clothes Rack. An Iron Pot Scrubber. Remove Fruit Stains. A Soap Shaker. A Kitchen Press. Drink for the Harvest Field. Box for Knives and Forks. Frame for Cooling Pies. A Small Toaster. Good and Bad Cooking. An Annex to Coffee Mills. Scouring Mitten. Cup for Sealing Wax. Tunnel Cake Pan. Wood Boxes. Convenient and Ornamental Wood-Boxes. Canning Tomatoes. Rat and Mouse Traps. An Unpatented Trap. Tomato Catsup – Tomato Sauce. Easily-Made Steps. Wooden Fruit Knives. Canning Fruit and Vegetables. Corn-Cob Crate. Heating Water—A Japan Bath. Strawberry Short-Cake. Egg-Tester.... ....

HOUSEHOLD CONVENIENCES.

CHAPTER I.

AROUND THE HOUSE.

FOOT SCRAPERS, OR BOOT CLEANERS.

Some people, men in particular, do not pay due attention to the removal of dirt from their boots and shoes, and often walk into a kitchen or sitting-room, upon a clean floor or carpet, with much mud and dirt adhering

Fig. 1.—A FOOT SCRAPER.

to their foot-gear. This may be prevented by placing a boot scraper or cleaner near the door, and in laying walks near the house and the barn, and other out-buildings. Any of the forms shown in figures 1 to 4 may be attached to the step at the door, or secured to a piece of board one inch thick, one foot wide, and about two feet in length. The scrapers shown in figures 1 and 2 are of iron, and attached by screws to the bottom piece. A blacksmith can bend an old piece of iron into the form desired. Figure 3 shows a piece of hard-wood, one foot in length, four inches wide, and nearly one inch thick, with one edge made quite sharp, the whole being nailed firmly to the end of a piece of board. The scraper shown in figure 4 consists of two wooden pins one inch in diameter, firmly secured in holes made in the bottom board near one end, three inches from which is a bar, *b*, either of

Fig. 2.   Fig. 3.   Fig. 4.

hard-wood or of iron, fastened upon the pins. This form has some advantages, as the tops of the pins, if made flat and sharp, will aid in cleaning the sides of the boots. A mat should be provided, and in absence of anything better, a piece of old carpet will serve a most excellent purpose. The house-keeper may need occasionally to refer the careless members of the family to the foot scraper and mat.

HOW A SCRAPER WAS MADE.

A scraper (figure 5) may be made out of an old spade,

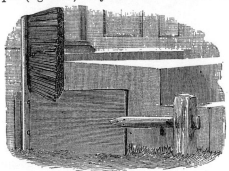

Fig. 5.—A GOOD MUD SCRAPER.

and the head of a worn-out broom. Remove a little of the mortar between the bricks of the house-wall, and fix the cutting end of the spade firmly in the crevice. Drive a short piece of timber a foot into the ground, and fasten the broken handle into the top of it with a nail. Then with two strong nails the old broom head is fixed to the wall, just above the spade. As all do not live in brick houses, two strips of wood, nailed perpendicularly to the house, and just far enough apart to hold the edge of the spade, would answer the same good purpose.

A PORTABLE SCRAPER AND MAT.

The bottom of the scraper, shown in figure 6, is a moderately heavy board, about ten inches wide, and thirty to thirty-six inches long. Near one end is attached a

Fig. 6.—PORTABLE SCRAPER AND MAT.

stout scraper, which any blacksmith can hammer out. At the other end of the board, and well out of the way of the scraper, is a coarse mat. This mat may be made of cocoa-nut fiber, such as are sold in the stores, or of common corn-husks, but whatever kind is used, it should be one that will stand hard usage, and is well fastened to the board. A very good mat for daily use may be made by boring inch-holes at regular intervals in a board, drawing through them tufts of doubled corn-husks, so that the ends will all be at one side, and then shearing off the ends of the husks, fairly even, but not too smooth. A board thus stuffed with husks, and nailed to the one that

holds the scraper, would answer. A scraper and rough
mat being provided, as here represented — and there
should be several of them—they should be placed some
distance from the house. Almost every farm-house is
surrounded by its garden, or front-yard, and in these
the walks are, or should be, in good order. Such a scraper and mat should be placed where the men leave the
fields or the barn-yard, and enter the better-kept surroundings of the house. If the scraper is placed at
some distance from the house, it will prevent much
mud from being brought to, and accumulating on,
the piazza and steps.

A MUD MAT.

Procure a few dozen of common inch square fence
pickets, three feet or more in length, and a few branches

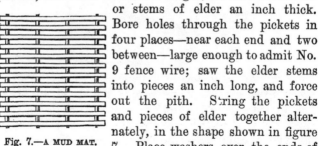

or stems of elder an inch thick.
Bore holes through the pickets in
four places—near each end and two
between—large enough to admit No.
9 fence wire; saw the elder stems
into pieces an inch long, and force
out the pith. String the pickets
and pieces of elder together alter-
nately, in the shape shown in figure

Fig. 7.—A MUD MAT.   7. Place washers over the ends of
the wires, and after cutting the ends the proper length,
rivet them down upon the washers. These mats may be
kept outside of the door-step, and if the boots are rubbed
upon them, the soles will be freed from much of the coarser
mud or earth adhering to them, and will not soil the
ordinary door mats nearly so much as without their use.

A SUMMER SUBSTITUTE FOR A CISTERN.

Many kitchens are without cisterns, and any suggestion regarding a substitute, by which a supply of rain-water can be had, if for only part of the time, will be gladly received by house-keepers. The substitute is an old "rain barrel." Usually this stands at the corner of the house, and to obtain water from it, women are obliged to go out of the kitchen. Place the barrel on a box or

Fig. 8.—SUBSTITUTE FOR A CISTERN.

other support near and level with the kitchen window. Insert a faucet in the lower part of the barrel, so that it can be easily reached from the open kitchen window. Have it so that the pail can be filled while it stands on the window-sill. It would be still more convenient, if the faucet could be inside the house, connecting with the barrel by a piece of gas-pipe.

A FILTER FOR A CISTERN.

Figure 9 shows a filter. It is a large barrel, with one end knocked out. At the bottom is a layer of fine charcoal, *d*. Above this is a layer of fine gravel, *c*, over this is a layer of coarse gravel, *b*, and on the top of the barrel is a thin strainer, *a*, held in place by a hoop which fits over the barrel. The cloth is depressed in the center, as seen in the cut. This strainer catches all leaves and coarse dirt, and should be cleaned after every shower. Some use a wire strainer of very fine mesh, but the cloth answers the purpose very well. The filtered water flows through a hole, *e*. Into this hole a metal tube a foot or more long, punched full of holes, and covered with wire netting, is inserted. Six inches below the top is another

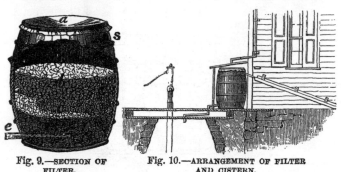

Fig. 9.—SECTION OF　　　Fig. 10.—ARRANGEMENT OF FILTER
FILTER.　　　　　　　　AND CISTERN.

hole, *s*, which is fitted with a short pipe. During a heavy shower the overflow runs out of this hole, and into a spout provided for it. Figure 10 shows the general arrangement of the entire apparatus. The barrel has a small shed built over it, to protect it from the sun and weather. This shed should open at one end, so the barrel can be taken out at any time. The top is movable, to allow the strainer to be cleaned. The lower section of the water-spout should be loose, so that it may be moved up or down, and turned. In figure 10, the elbow rests on a block, or bracket, and the water flows into the barrel through a hole in the cover of the shed. When the cistern is full, the elbow is turned, and drops down to a block, and throws the water into the spout, to be carried away, or into a "wash water" cistern near by. The above arrangement may be modified to suit different circumstances and places. When rain water is used exclusively for cooking and drinking, it is best to have a cistern for it alone, and a separate one for wash water.

RAIN-WATER STRAINER.

During every brisk shower the roofs of buildings are washed clean, and if the water is allowed to flow directly

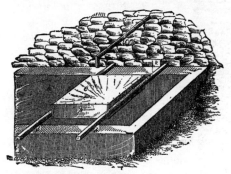

Fig. 11.—STRAINER FOR CISTERN.

into the cistern, much dust, dirt, leaves, etc., is carried with it to render the water impure. At the beginning of a storm, it is well to let the rain wash the roof for an hour or two before the stream is allowed to enter the cistern. This is especially necessary where pigeons and other birds collect upon the roofs. The inlet pipe should be so arranged that the first of the rain water will run to waste, and the balance be conducted to the cistern, and this without attention, during each shower. Figure 11 shows a portable strainer, consisting of a box, *p*, three feet square and four inches deep. A bit of coarse cloth is tacked to the upper edge; this will allow water to pass quite rapidly, and should be six inches lower at the center than at the sides. Supports or handles, *b, b,* are attached to the sides, the ends

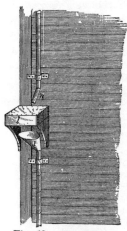

Fig. 12.—STRAINER FOR WATER PIPE.

of which rest upon the walls of the cistern, *h.* The inlet pipe, *r,* discharges immediately upon the cloth *e,* which retains all leaves, coarse dirt, etc. This cloth should be cleaned three or four times per year, which is easily done by placing the box, *p,* bottom up and dashing water upon the cloth. The strainer described is for a cistern located in the cellar and easily accessible. The strainer shown in figure 12 is for use in the side pipe. The manner of constructing is fully shown in the engraving. It is best located about five feet from the ground, or within easy reach. The box, *l,* is eighteen inches square and six inches deep. The strainer should be depressed about one foot that it may not overflow during heavy showers. The box should be easily removed for cleaning the strainer, etc. In either plan, to prevent the water from dashing too violently upon the cloth, it should run upon a sieve or something to retard the fall and divide the stream.

THE WASTES OF COUNTRY HOUSES.

The disposal of the wastes of a country house is of as much importance as that of a house in the city—in fact more so, as there is no general system of sewers like those in cities, and each house must provide for itself. Many a neat looking country house rarely has its front door opened, and when it is opened, it is, alas, too often to allow a little coffin to be carried out; the neighbors who have gathered in a sympathizing manner, talk in an undertone of diphtheria, scarlet fever, and reverently speak of the "dispensations of Providence." Were these neighbors to go around to the back door, they would perhaps find its surroundings—just like their own. The kitchen slops have been, ever since the house was built,

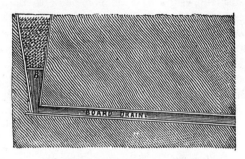

Fig. 13.—CROSS SECTION OF DRAIN.

thrown out from the door. The kitchen sink may empty its contents in a shallow drain, which leads nowhere, but the water soaks away as it may, and in either case the soil all around the rear of the house is reeking with slop water. No healthy growth of tree or plant can be had here, and what is worse still, the well is usually not far off. As there is a reciprocal relation between all the members of the body, so there is a direct relation between the back door and the occasional melancholy openings of the front door. There is no problem—such as the simple one of two and two make four—more thoroughly fixed and established, than that the health of the family, whether in the costly city mansion or in the humblest cottage or log cabin, depends upon the manner in which the wastes of the family occupying the mansion or cabin are disposed of.

Provide a cess-pool in a suitable place, and a tight drain to take all liquids to it. The cess-pool should be

at least forty feet from either house or well. Make it large, as the larger it is, the longer it will last. A quick method is to get a

Fig. 14.—TOP OF FUNNEL. large cask, which need not be tight; such as hardware comes in will answer. Knock out both heads, and dig a hole deep enough to hold it; of course, provided the soil is loose and sandy. Place the headless cask in the hole, with its top at least three feet below the surface. Into this place all the accumulated stones, bricks, and such material that may be at hand, to at least half fill it. Connect the drain with it, lay some stout planks across the top, and cover them with earth. In order to make repairs if needed, take the direction and distance from some permanent point, so that the cess-pool may be readily found.

The drain may be made of boards, six inches wide and free from knots; they are to be nailed together to form a square drain, using tar, or thick paint, at the joints. If the interior has several coats of oil or crude petroleum, it will be all the more durable. To receive the slops, a long and narrow funnel should be made as in figure 13. This is about fourteen inches square at the top, and tapers below to the size of the drain. A piece of plank, in which numerous half-inch holes are bored, is placed at B, above which the funnel is filled with small stones. The upper end of the funnel has a square frame projecting about four inches above the surface as in figure 14. The waste water is to be poured into this frame, and the small stones will arrest all solid matters, and prevent them from passing into the drain. It may be desirable to have the kitchen sink discharge into the drain, the funnel of which may be in this case quite near the house, as shown in figure 15. It is well to cover the top of the drain with a screen of wire. It has been assumed that the sole object is to get rid of the house slops. If these are to be used in the garden, the cess-pool should be located with reference to this end, and it must be made water-tight, with its top well below the reach of frost.

Fig. 15.—DISCHARGE PIPE AT SIDE OF HOUSE.

In some soils, an excavation of the desired size may have its bottom and sides covered by a coat of cement plastered directly upon them. Where the soil is not sufficiently firm to admit of this, the walls and bottom must be bricked and made water-tight by a coating of cement. The top should be covered with strong planks. A pump may be arranged to raise the contents of the cess-pool, which may be conveyed to every part of the garden by cheap troughs, made of two boards nailed together, and one season's increased produce will repay all outlay.

MAKE YOUR OWN HAMMOCK.

A pretty and very comfortable hammock can be made
of awning-cloth. Two pieces, six feet long and a little
over a yard wide, are cut for the bottom of the hammock;
and two strips, five inches wide, to go along the sides.
These are scalloped and bound with worsted braid, and
the strips basted in place between the two large pieces.
The side seams are sewed up on the wrong side. After

Fig. 16.—A HOME-MADE HAMMOCK.

being turned right side out, the two ends are bound with
braid. Eight curtain rings are sewed on each end, and
to each ring is fastened a heavy hammock cord. These
cords are all joined to a large iron ring, as shown in
figure 16. To hang the hammock, a light rope is passed
through the rings and around two trees or posts.

A hammock should be hung where there is a good
afternoon shade, and if intended in part for children's
use should be hung so low that small children can get
into it by the aid of a box or low stool, and over soft
ground, so that the numerous tumbles that are probable

will be harmless. If no other place is available, it may be
hung between the pillars of a shady veranda, a place well
enough for the older people who use it, but undesirable
for children, on account of the lack of a soft turf, as well
as for the noise which accompanies its use by the young-
sters. When children are only to use the hammock, the
manner of hanging it is not important, but if provided
for the use of grown persons, it should then be so sus-

Fig. 17.—HOW TO SLING A HAMMOCK.

pended that the head will always be considerably higher
than the foot, and much of the comfort of the one
who uses this, depends upon a proper observance of
this fact. Figure 17 shows a hammock suspended from
the columns of a veranda. The hook which supports the
head end, is six and one-fourth feet from the floor, and
that for the foot end is three and three-fourths feet, and
these proportions should be observed wherever it may be
hung, to secure the most desirable curve for the ease of
the occupant. Another point to be observed; the head

end is fastened to the hook by a rope less than a foot long—just enough to properly attach it, while at the foot is a rope four and a half feet long. This gives the greatest freedom for swinging the lower part of the body, while the head moves but little. This is a point which cannot be observed in a hammock for children, who think more of it as a swing than as a place for comfortable repose. When trees serve for supports, ample provision should be made to prevent injury to the bark, by means of stout canvas or heavy bagging between the ropes to which it is suspended and the bark. If the hanging be so arranged that the hammock can be taken in during long storms, it will last much longer.

A HOME-MADE TENT.

It is easy to make a tent which, if not as pleasing in outline as those for sale in the stores, casts quite as grateful a shadow, and is fully as comfortable. The first thing needed, is a light but firm frame, put up in a substantial manner. The cover is made of awning cloth, and just large enough to fit easily over the frame. The top is in one piece, and to it are sewed the side pieces and those for the ends, cut in scallops around the lower edge and bound with woollen braid, of a color to correspond with that of the stripe in the cloth. The pieces must all be sewed together very firmly, and the seams bound on the wrong side. Cords are attached to each corner of the cover, by which it is tied to the frame. If the tent is to stand in a very exposed situation, where there is an entire absence of shade, an extra curtain will be desirable. This should be supplied with rings, and hung on the side needing the protection from the sun. It should be as wide as the tent, and long enough to reach the ground. Two frames may be put up; one on that part of the lawn which is most pleasant in the morning, and the other in a favorite after-dinner gathering place. If the frames are

Fig. 18.—A CHEAP LAWN TENT.

of the same size, one cover will do for both. In this way, two tents can be made with but little more trouble and expense than one. A tent as above described is shown in figure 18.

A SHADED GARDEN SEAT.

Figure 19 shows a garden seat with a tent-like roof. A shaded seat of some kind is found very useful by those who have croquet grounds, as well as by others who wish to enjoy sewing or reading in the open air, and cannot avail themselves of the shade of trees. The top of the one figured is made to incline backwards or forwards, as may be required. It would not take much contrivance to fit up a light awning that would be quite as useful if not so elegant as this. Where the seat is to remain stationary,

Fig. 19.—A SHADED GARDEN SEAT.

the awning may be supported by stout poles driven firmly into the ground.

WINDOW SCREENS AND AWNINGS.

No house in this country can be regarded as appropriately designed unless it has broad and abundant verandas or piazzas. Windows in the upper stories, and not otherwise protected, must have separate shades or screens. The usual inside muslin screen mounted on rollers, affords shade, but it excludes air. Out-side screens, or awnings, are better than these, as they shade the room and allow the lower part of the window to be open. These awnings, attached to the window-frame above, and below to an iron rod bent twice at right angles, and projecting outward, are far more pleasant than any inside arrangement can be. Besides this, they give the

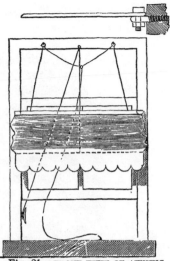

Fig. 20.—AWNING, SIDE VIEW.   Fig. 21.—FRONT VIEW OF AWNING.

house a cool and airy

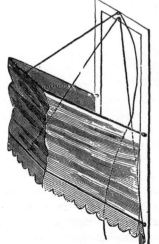

Fig. 22.—IMPROVED AWNING.

appearance, a point not to be despised, as it is well to have the house look comfortable as well as be so. Still awnings of this kind have the disadvantage that they prevent all proper circulation of air through the upper part of the window. Figure 20 shows an awning so arranged that it can be let down from the top. The upper edge of the canvas is fastened to a light wooden bar, which is drawn up by a cord that passes over a small pulley at the top of the window casing. It is let down by loosening the fastening of the cord, when the top

of the awning falls of its own weight.   Figure 21 shows
a front view of this same arrangement.   An easy way of
securing the hinge motion at the lower fastening of the
awning to the wall, is shown at the top of the figure.
The eye of the end of the iron frame and that of the screw
are held side by side by a small bolt.   Another plan is
the one given in figure 22, where there is an iron frame

Fig. 23.—AN AWNING FOR A DOORWAY.

for the top of the awning similar to the one at the bottom.

An elaborate awning with patent iron frame, etc.,
to be· lowered and raised at pleasure, differs very ma-
terially in cost from the one shown in figure 23.   This
latter can easily be made at home; it has only a stationary wooden frame, it is true, but it answers the
purpose just as well as a more expensive and pretentious
affair.   A square frame is made of strips of wood, and
fastened firmly to the side of the house, a little above the

door or window, with another wooden strip to hold
it in place, reaching from the house to each of the front
corners of the frame. The awning is wide-stripe bed-
ticking (or awning-cloth if preferred), and the top and
front are all in one. This requires two or more widths
of material, and the side pieces are cut to fit, and sewed
on. The lower edge is scalloped out all round, and bound
with bright-colored braid, and the whole is tacked closely
and firmly to the frame. This awning is durable as well
as ornamental, and need not be taken down all summer.

A CLOTHES-LINE REEL.

Figures 24 and 25 show a cheap clothes-line reel. A
box was procured from the store—a starch-box well made

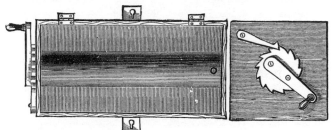

Fig. 24.—INTERIOR OF CLOTHES-LINE   Fig. 25.—CRANK AND
REEL.   PAWL.

—about eighteen inches long by eight inches wide and
high. A turned shaft about an inch and a half in
diameter, and the length of the box, is placed in a hole
cut in one end of the box the size of the shaft, the other
end of the shaft coming up flush with the inside of the
box and held in place by a large screw. The opposite end
of the shaft has a ratchet wheel of wood, with a crank
fastened to the shaft by two long screws. A pawl of wood
engages the wheel and holds the line taut. There is a

2

hole in one end of the shaft large enough for the line to pass through, it being fastened by a knot tied in one end. On the back is a strip one inch thick, two inches wide, and about two inches longer than the width of the box, with slots in the ends to hang the reel upon two large screws in the side of the house, or other convenient place. The cover is fastened on with two butts on the lower side, and turns down out of the way when the reel is used. The construction of the reel is given in figure 24, and figure 25 shows the ratchet wheel with the crank and the pawl.

ANOTHER CLOTHES-LINE REEL.

In the first place, there is an upright box, to serve as a post, built of boards; this is shown at A in figure 26, being a front view, and figure 27 a side view in section. This box, A, is made large enough for the weight, B, to move up and down freely inside of it. Attached to this upright box, at the proper hight, is a box, C, to contain the reel for the line. The reel is double; it has a large shaft, D, upon which the line is wound, and a smaller shaft, E, for the cord of the weight. This box is so attached to the upright one, that the small shaft, E, is opposite to it. The weight has a pulley attached, and the cord for the weight, fastened to the top of the upright box, goes through the pulley on the weight, over a pulley at the top, and down to the shaft, E, of the wheel. When this cord enters the box there is a guide pulley or roller, F, to make it run smoothly. When the line is put upon the reel, the weight is first wound up by revolving the reel, which will wind the weight-cord up upon E. The line being made fast to the shaft D, the weight is allowed to run down, which will reel up the line upon D. There must be an opening in the box, C, the length of the shaft, *D*, in order to allow the line to run freely. When the clothes-line is pulled out, of course the weight will be wound up, and, when it is to be taken in, the

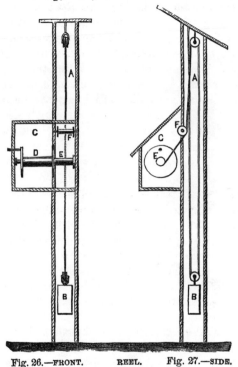

Fig. 26.—FRONT.　　REEL.　　Fig. 27.—SIDE.

descent of the weight will cause the line to be reeled upon its shaft and be properly housed.

A THIRD FORM OF REEL.

Figure 28 shows a large wooden spool with an axle or journals; the spool is about six inches, and the journals about one inch in diameter. The spool is about four inches long, while the side axle is but one inch. The ends of the axle rest in small holes in the sides of the upright support. A small strong cord is fastened to and around the journal, and there is attached to the cord

Fig. 28.—REEL AND BIRD-HOUSE.

a weight of about six pounds. A common cotton or hemp clothes line of proper length is fastened by one end to the spool, and at the other end has an iron ring, or a stick will answer. When the weight falls three inches, the spool will revolve once, and wind up eighteen inches of the line; if it falls five feet it will wind up thirty feet of the line. For convenience, both the clothes line and that carrying the weight are shown wound up. In use when the clothes line is wound up on the spool, the weighted line will be unwound, and the weight at the floor. To stretch the line, take hold of the ring and walk to the point where it is to be attached; this will unwind the line and wind up the weight. When the clothes are taken down, unhitch the line, and the descent of the weight will wind it up at once, and it will be housed without trouble. The spool may be placed in any convenient shed or out-building, or a column may be constructed for it which will at the same time answer as a support for a bird house, as in the engraving.

A CLOTHES LINE HOLDER.

An improved clothes post, by which the line when filled can be raised, and the use of props or clothes poles is rendered unnecessary, may be made as shown in figure 29. Posts are set in the usual manner, and an arm, *C*, is fastened to the top by a strong bolt. The arm should be four or five feet long, with the outer part longer than the inner part. The line, *D*, is fastened to the inner part of the arm, loose enough to allow for tightening. A cord, *B*, is fixed to the outer end of the arm, and a

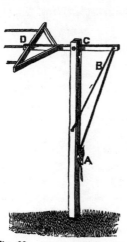
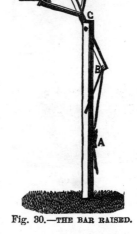

Fig. 29.—CLOTHES LINE BAR.   Fig. 30.—THE BAR RAISED.

hole or hook is placed at the post. By pulling down the outer end of the arm, the line is raised, and held by drawing the cord tightly and passing it a few times around the cleat, *A*, as shown in the engraving.

A CLOTHES LINE ELEVATOR.

The elevator, figure 31, consists of a plank post, *a*, projecting four feet above ground, to which is bolted at the top, near one edge, a lever, *R*, five feet in length.

The end of the clothes line is attached two feet from the bolt.   The opposite end, three feet in length, is used for a handle or lever for adjusting the clothes line, when filled with clothes, and is retained in position by a wooden button, *B*. A small block is nailed upon the post at *P*, to hold the lever in a horizontal position, while the clothes are being placed upon and removed from the line.

Fig. 31.—ELEVATOR FOR CLOTHES LINE.

A similar "elevator" may be placed at each end of the clothes line, and it may be made of any desired size.

A REVOLVING CLOTHES LINE.

In towns and villages, where space must be economized, and where the demands of the garden will not allow of a wide space for the clothes yard, some contrivance for drying clothes within a small area becomes necessary. Various devices, in the way of clothes driers, have been invented and patented, but they are not essentially superior to the one here given. This is designed for the regular family washing, and is to be set up in a convenient place in the yard. Any one of fair ingenuity can contrive a similar affair, to be used in a spare room in winter, in times when clothes will not dry out of doors. This revolving clothes drier, shown in figure 32, may be easily made by any one familiar with tools in half a day, from the following directions: A wooden hub, *B*, eight to ten inches in diameter, is mortised with six holes, for

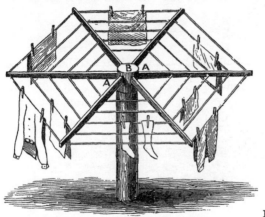

Fig. 32.—REVOLVING CLOTHES DRIER.

Fig. 33.—POST FOR DRIER.

the reception of the arms, *A, A;* these are from five to seven feet in length, seven feet being sufficient to hold the washing for a large family. It will be found less work to simply bore six two-inch holes in the hub *B*, and round the end of arms *A*. Give the ends of these a good coat of paint, and drive them firmly into the hub. Small holes are bored, from eight to ten inches apart, the whole length of the arms, excepting for fifteen inches of each arm nearest the hub. The clothes line is tightly strung through the holes; a white wire clothes line is preferable, as it will outlast a dozen hemp or cotton ones. The standard (figure 33) is simply a common post

set firmly in the ground; in the top of this is driven, as
a pintle, a round iron bar, an inch and one-fourth in
diameter, and left projecting six inches; this fits in the
hole in the hub. These holes should be so bored
that the outer end of each arm will be from eight to
twelve inches higher than the hub. When hanging out
clothes, so soon as one section is filled, revolve the line a
few feet, and when that is filled, continue the operation;
this avoids travelling along the line in the snow, wet
grass, etc.

A SIDE-SHELF FOR DRAINING BOTTLES.

Bottles for holding fruit, catsup, etc., should, when
emptied of their contents, be thoroughly dried and aired,

Fig. 34.—SIDE-SHELF FOR BOTTLES.

after being well washed and rinsed, or when they are
refilled the fruit will not keep well. It is a hazardous
task to stand bottles up on a table to drain, especially the
long, slender ones so often used for holding catsup, for
the least jar may send them over and break them. Besides, when stood up on a table, although they will be
well drained, the air is not free to circulate through
them. A simple little contrivance, shown in figure 34,
overcomes both difficulties. It is a board four feet long
and fifteen inches wide, in which are two dozen various
sized holes, the largest of sufficient diameter to admit the
mouth of a good-sized fruit jar, and the smallest large

enough to hold the slender necks of catsup bottles. The board is fastened to the wall on a south porch by hinges. Twine strings pass through holes in each end of the board, and fastened to staples in the wall, hold the shelf in place at the right angle. When not wanted, the shelf can be hooked up against the wall; but this is seldom necessary, for when not in use in holding bottles, it makes a temporary resting place for such articles as partly ripened tomatoes and seeds.

A FOLDING TABLE FOR A PORCH.

Various kinds of work, such as preparing vegetables and fruit, ironing, and sometimes the necessary scouring

Fig. 35.—THE TABLE IN POSITION.

of tin things, can be done as well on a shady, protected porch as in the kitchen, and with much more comfort, for it affords a pleasant retreat from the heat of the indispensable cooking stove. The table (fig. 35) is made of pine, three feet long by two and a half feet wide. The top is firmly fastened to the wall by two strong hinges. The support in front is nearly a foot wide, fastened on with a large hinge, so that when the table is in use, it is upright, and even with the front edge. When not in use, the table is hooked up against the house wall, as shown in figure 36, and is entirely out of the way. Such a table might also be found very convenient in a small

kitchen, as it could be let down when any extra work required a second table, and be easily put back when not needed. Any one who has not yet the desirable addition of a back porch to the house, will find a folding table put up against the side of the house near the kitchen

Fig. 36.—THE TABLE FOLDED.

door very useful in pleasant weather, as shown in figure 35. This table should be on the shaded side.

A SIMPLE ASH-SIFTER.

In no well-managed family is a waste of coal allowed, but the ashes are separated from the cinders, and all of these that can be burned are utilized. Sifting coal ashes is generally a disagreeable job, and it is not to be wondered at that servants shirk it, when allowed to, yet by proper arrangements the labor can be greatly reduced, and the work done rapidly and neatly. Figure 37 shows an ash-sifter with one side removed, to expose the interior arrangement. No measurements are given, because it may be built in a wood-shed or other out-building, and will be of a size to suit the place, or the amount of work required of it. The sifter consists of an inclined sieve—the wire-cloth for which may be had of the desired fineness at the hardware stores—placed at such an angle that the cinders will roll down of their own weight, while the ashes will fall through the meshes of the sieve. This sieve, *C*, is enclosed on all sides, and is provided with a receptacle, *B,* for the ashes, as they come from the grate; one, *D,* for the sifted ashes, and another, *E,* for the cinders freed from the ashes. Its working is automatic; the material to be sifted, being put in at *B,* will slide down the sieve, until stopped by an accumulation of cinders at *E,* but on removing these the sifting will go on again. The ashes must be removed as they accumulate at *D,* or the sifter may be placed where the ashes will

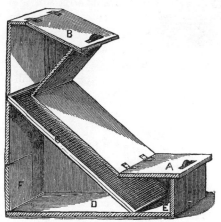

Fig. 37.—AN ASH-SIFTER.

pass down through the floor, or out at one side, of their own weight. Those who use the ashes in earth-closets, will prefer the construction shown in the engraving, in which they are kept dry and ready for use, when needed.

A BARREL ASH-SIFTER.

To make the sifter shown in figure 38, bore holes near one end of any old barrel, place two stout wires across and tightly clinch them upon the outside; these make a firm rest for a sieve. Midway between the cross wires on one

side, make a slot in the barrel large enough for a handle, which is an inch through, and fastened to the top edges of the sieve, notches having been first made in the handle to fit the sieve. Provide a cover, and the sifter is ready for use. The ashes are put into the sieve, which, by means of the handle, is to be briskly shaken back and forth. This sifter is easily made, and cheap, and

Fig. 38.—A BARREL ASH-SIFTER.

if the cover fits fairly on the top, there will be little or no dust in the operation.

A SAFE ASH-BIN.

Many fires, sometimes most disastrous ones, are traced to the method of disposing of ashes; and no wonder, when so few families have any safe place for depositing them, even if they have iron pails for carrying them. Very often they are left in the pail in a wooden out-building, or thrown into a corner of a wooden smoke house, under the impression that there are no live coals in them. Hard-wood charcoal buried in ashes will hold fire a long time. Farmers having a smoke house, if they burn wood, dump the ashes in one corner of it, to save them for soap-making, or as a fertilizer. But the large majority in both village and country, throw their ashes in a heap on the ground. A little expense would provide a perfectly fire-proof bin or house that will keep the ashes fresh and dry. Figure 39 shows a convenient form. It is built of brick, is about five feet long, four feet wide, and four feet high, outside measurement. If the soil is sandy or well drained, the bottom may be a foot below the surface. The roof is made of boards lined with tin or sheet iron—old stove pipes opened out flat will answer. One side is

Fig. 39.—A CHEAP AND SAFE ASH BIN.

hung on hinges at the ridge, answering for a door. A single course of bricks, making the wall four and a half inches thick, is sufficiently strong. Old brick will answer, and it may be as plain or as ornamental as desired. It may be built of stone, if these are at hand, and can be used more cheaply than brick. Usually, brick will be most economical, on account of the saving of work and mortar.

A WATER GUARD TO A WINDOW BRUSH.

When windows are washed with a long-handled scrubbing brush or broom, there is often great discomfort aris-

Fig. 40.—A GUARD FOR A WINDOW BRUSH.

ing from the suds and water running down the brush handle and upon the hands and clothing of the operator.

This can be avoided by a simple device shown in figure 40. It consists of a ring of stout leather, cut to fit closely upon the handle, and placed a foot or so below the head of the brush or broom. The water coming down the handle meets with the lateral surface of the ring, and is carried off on one side towards the window and away from the person using the brush. A similar ring of rubber would answer a like purpose. It is a small affair, but the ease and comfort of much domestic labor depends upon attention to trifles.

WOOD RACK AND WOOD APRON.

Figure 41 shows two convenient methods of carrying fire wood. A wood rack for the shoulder is made of a

Fig. 41.—WOOD RACK AND APRON.

piece of round hard-wood, with four long pins set in the upper side. These pins are placed in V-shaped pairs, between which the fire wood is piled. A handle, three feet long, is set in a hole bored in the center of the under side of the body of the rack. This device, when complete, resembles a "skeleton" hod, and is carried in the same manner as a hod for brick or mortar. A second method of carrying wood consists of a stout canvas "apron," in the lower part of which the fuel is placed, as shown in the engraving. A boy, or other person, with much wood to move short distances, will find either of these devices labor-saving, and they are quickly made.

THE DISPOSAL OF HOUSE SLOPS.

The premises around the back door of a farm or country house should be kept as clean and neat as those at the

Fig. 42.—A SLOP BARREL.

front door. To accomplish this is the difficulty. Where no provision is made by means of a sink and proper drainage, to carry off the waste water of a house, it will always be thrown by servants and others in the most "convenient" spot, and this is usually about the back door. We can hardly expect girls to carry waste slops any distance on a cold day, particularly to empty them on a manure heap. Provide a good-sized cask mounted on wheels in summer, and on runners in winter, which can be drawn

up for use not far from the back door. Into this the
slops can be thrown, and when necessary, the whole
may be drawn to the proper spot, easily emptied, and
returned to its place for future use. The cask should be
hung by means of pivots in such a manner that it can be
easily upset, and when released will return to a perpendicular position. Placing the pivots slightly above the
center of the cask on each side will do this. A slop barrel thus arranged is shown in figure 42. It may be used
in a garden to carry water about in dry seasons.

THE HOME CREMATORY.

When one who has lived in a city removes to the
country, he soon misses several of the conveniences necessary to a dense population. One of the most prominent
of these is the scavenger's or dustman's cart, which in
well-regulated cities and towns comes around at stated
intervals to carry away the household wastes. These
wastes, known by the comprehensive name of rubbish,
occur in a country house as well as in a city residence,
and are more noticeable for the reason that there is no
provision for their removal. A large share of the family
wastes may be made useful, so to speak, by destroying
them, that is, by burning, by which all that is of any
value will be left in the form of ashes. Every country
place, large or small, should afford some corner in which
a crematory, or "burn heap," may be located. The
wastes of a household are of three classes : The utterly
useless and incombustible, such as old crockery and
stone ware, old iron vessels, fruit cans, etc., which are
best disposed of by burying in a deep hole; then there
are the weeds, vegetable refuse of the garden, and other

materials that will decompose, which may be turned to good account in the pig-pen or on the manure heap ; still a third class comprises materials which cannot be readily converted into manure, and are too valuable to bury. Of this kind are all clippings and prunings of trees and shrubs, all weeds too far advanced for the manure heap on account of their seeds, old stakes and labels which are of no further use, waste paper and other combustibles that accumulate in the house, and various other materials. We find it convenient to have a barrel in a suitable place to receive all waste paper and such rubbish as would be scattered if placed upon the heap at once, and the best disposition to make of otherwise useless barrels is, to consign them to the heap with their contents. If such rubbish is occasionally compacted by pounding it down, using a heavy stake as a pounder, a barrel will hold a surprising quantity. At a convenient time such accumulations should be burned, of course, taking all proper precautions against burning anything else. It may be sometimes necessary to add combustible materials as fuel, in order that all the contents of the heap may be thoroughly burned and reduced to ashes. It is to be kept in mind that, the chief end and object of this method, aside from getting rid of the rubbish, is the ashes. Hence the heap, instead of covering a wide area, should be kept with as small a base as possible, and care taken to secure thorough burning. Soon after the fire is out, the ashes should be taken up; never mind if some soil is mixed with them, and placed in barrels or boxes for future use. Do not take these receptacles to a shed or other outbuilding, as there is always danger of hidden fire, but protect them from rain by covering with old boards. There is no crop, upon old lands at least, whether of the farm, orchard, vegetable, or other garden, that will not be benefited by an application of ashes. Now that wood is but little used for fuel, this valuable fertilizer is an-

nually becoming more rare and difficult to procure.   By
proper attention in the direction here indicated, a surprisingly large quantity of ashes may be secured, while
much unsightly rubbish is disposed of.   We would add
that, as a rule, the best method of utilizing all large bones
is, to place them on the heap and allow their ashes to add
to the fertilizing value of the rest.

AN EASILY MADE HAND SNOW-PLOW.

Clearing the paths and shovelling off the snow is a job
that generally belongs to the boys of the family, and while

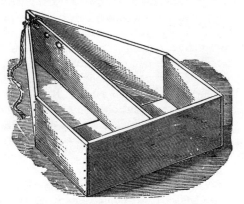

Fig. 43.—HOME-MADE PATH-CLEANER.

a snow-plow is hardly a household implement, the results
of its use are of so much importance to the household
generally, that we give it here.   Upon every place of sufficient size to warrant it, there should be a snow-plow,
drawn by a horse ; but a hand-plow is a great help, especially if used while the snow is still light and dry.   To

make it, take a box thirty inches long by fifteen wide, and ten deep. One side of the box is removed, and a strip of board thirty-six inches long and ten wide is placed through the center and braced by two pieces, each thirty inches long and ten wide, which are nailed to this center-board and the ends of the box, as seen in figure 43. Holes are bored near the top edge of the center-board, to allow the rope to be attached by which the plow is drawn. The box will fill with snow, which will give it sufficient weight.

LEACHES, LYE, AND SOAP.

Where soap is to be made from ashes, the first step is to extract their soluble parts, to get a solution of

Fig. 44.—A V-SHAPED LEACH.

them in water, known as lye. To do this, the ashes are placed in some receptacle, called a leach, in which water can gradually trickle through them, and come out below as a strong solution or lye. Figure 44 shows the old-fashion V-shaped leach. There is a frame of two by three-inch scantling, about a foot from the top, which is stayed by side pieces; the bottom is a log, in which a gutter is dug, to convey the lye to a pail, or other receptacle, placed at its lower end. The manner in which the leach is supported, and the arrangements of its sideboards, is sufficiently shown in the engraving. Sometimes an old sugar or molasses hogshead, obtainable cheaply at the store, is used as a leach. The hogshead, first having half-inch holes bored in its lower staves and ends, is set up, as shown in figure 45, upon a grooved plank, which will convey the lye to a vessel placed to receive it. This is kept in proper position by a frame, or by braces at the sides.

The old method of setting the leach was to place some bricks or stones in the bottom, next some brush, and over

Fig. 45.—USING A HOGSHEAD AS A LEACH.

this a layer of straw, and then shovel in the ashes. It is much easier and better to place on the bottom of the leach, of whatever kind, a piece of old blanket, or old carpet. This will prevent the ashes from clogging up the holes, and allow the lye to flow out. Ashes moisten slowly, and in filling the leach, it is better to place in a small quantity at a time, moistening each layer as it is placed in, and compacting it with a pounder of some kind. If the ashes are thus moistened all through, the leach will work more evenly than when filled dry. It is customary to make in the top of the ashes a cavity large enough to hold a pailful or two of water, and replenish the water as it soaks away. The more slowly the water percolates among the ashes, the stronger the lye will be. It is a common practice to place lime in the leach, six or eight quarts of quick lime being placed on the first layer of ashes. This makes the lye much stronger, the lime, it is stated, converting the carbonate of potash, as it exists in the ashes, in part into caustic potash.

A SCREEN AT THE HOUSE.

It is especially the case in sparsely settled portions of the country, that the house is placed quite near the pub-

Fig. 46.—SCREEN FOR A BACK YARD.

lic road. This is done to avoid a sense of loneliness, and to allow the inmates a glimpse of the few passers by, that they may not feel quite isolated. It generally happens that this advantage, as it is regarded, is offset by the exposure of the rear of the house, the back-door, and the back-door yard, to the gaze of all who pass, and

it becomes desirable to shut off this view of the premises
by a screen, which is necessary also to allow the inmates
to pass to the dairy-house, wood-shed, or other out-buildings, unobserved.   Houses, where it can be afforded, are
often provided with screens of lattice-work, of two-inch
slats, crossing one another, with a bottom board below,
painted white, while the lattice itself is green.   Such a
screen, while well enough in a village, is quite too artificial and conspicuous for a country home.   The best
screen for the country, whether for shutting out the
view, or for the shelter it affords, is a living one of evergreen trees.   This, however, can not be had at once—
time is required to produce it, and while this is growing
some other may be supplied.   The design shown in figure
46, has posts seven or eight feet high, which are connected by a cap-piece of boards, cut as there shown, and
strands of galvanized iron wire (No. 12 or 14), are passed
from post to post, every twelve or eighteen inches, according to the kind of plant to be used.   One of the
best plants for such a screen is a rampant growing grape-
vine, such as the Clinton, or Taylor, and until this
gets established, some annuals, as morning-glories, or
such quick-growing plants as the Madeira-vine may be
used.

A CARRIAGE STEP.

Few people ever know of the convenience of a carriage
step.   A man thinks such a convenience unnecessary
so far as he is concerned, and it is not considered part
of a woman's business to see to the construction of a
carriage step.   It should be built in a convenient place
in the garden fence near to the entrance gate.   It then
remains a part of the fence, and no injurious animal

can gain access by it to the garden. The steps are inside of the grounds, and a neat hand-rail should be

Fig. 47.—A CARRIAGE-STEP.

made on each side of it. Figure 47, so clearly explains itself that no further description is needed.

A WORK-STAND FOR THE LAWN.

Ladies who take their chairs to the lawn often find it inconvenient to keep their sewing—their work-basket, etc.—within reach. An ordinary stand or table is too large to carry out, besides, it will often be very unsteady from the irregularities in the lawn. A cheap and convenient substitute for a table can be made in the following manner: A good hard-wood stick is procured, one end of which is shaved down to a sharp point, figure 48; upon the other end two cleats are nailed—the shape of the cleats, and manner of fastening them, is explained by figures 49 and 50. In figure 51 is shown a cross-sectional view of the top of the stand, which consists of a

round board, with cleats so nailed upon the bottom that
they will fit as a dovetail upon the cleats on the upper
end of the stake. The stand and basket are shown in
position in figure 52. It is more convenient to have the
top so it can be easily taken from the stake, as it will then
occupy but a small place when not in use. It is well to

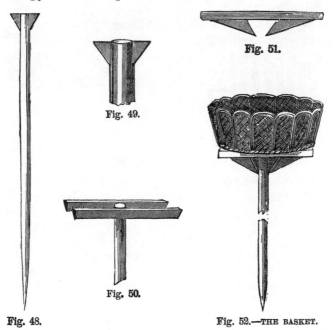

Fig. 51.

Fig. 49.

Fig. 50.

Fig. 48.

Fig. 52.—THE BASKET.

have a cord passing from the top to some place on the
stake, to always keep the two parts together. The whole
stand is very light ; can be easily taken out, and is set
by a thrust of the sharp end of the stake into the ground,
after which the top is put upon the cleats. It can be
placed close to the chair, will not upset, and occupies
but little space. The cost is but a trifle, and a boy
can make the stand.

VINES AT THE DOOR.

If the house-mother (to borrow a most convenient word from the Germans) looks after no other portion of the gardening, she is quite sure to take an interest in the vines, which cluster so closely around the door and windows that they seem a part of the house rather than of the garden.   Here is a common ground on which all can meet—the decoration of the house—for there is no work of the architect, however costly, but seems to need the final finish of vines, and no house, however poor in its exterior, but may be made to look home-like by the use of climbers.   In our climate every house should have a veranda of some sort, even if but a mere porch, to shelter the door; and whether it be an extended veranda or narrow "stoop," there is a place for vines.   The utility of vines, whether on the score of shade or that of mere ornament, needs no showing, as all will admit it, and it becomes merely a question of ways and means—what to plant, and how to grow it.   If there is neither veranda or porch, and most log houses, and some of more pretentions have neither, one need not be without vines.   A trellis of poles of some kind can be arranged to support the vines, and if it can be made of cedar and permanent, all the better; but if this can not be commanded, draw upon the stock of bean-poles, or get poles by some means that will answer for a season.   Given poles, a few nails, some wire and string, and assuming the rather improbable case that she can get no help, the woman can have the door shaded if she will.   As to the trellis, but a few suggestions need be given.   No matter if it looks rude at first, the vines will charitably cover any sins of construction.   Recollect that vines are heavy and autumn winds powerful; so regard strength rather than beauty. If there are two doors and but one trellis, set it at the one where it will be of the most use and comfort.   Of vines

3

we have both annual and perennial. Annuals raised each
year from seed are the least satisfactory, but are sometimes the only ones available. The number of those
which grow sufficiently tall is small. One of the best is
a native, the wild balsam-apple, or wild cucumber
(*Echinocystis*). But unfortunately this is not to be had
at the seed-stores, and unless you happen to know a
friend who has some seeds, this is out of the question.
Next comes the morning-glory, old, but good; the flowers are short-lived, but some of the finer kinds are sufficiently beautiful to offset this defect. A paper of seeds
of the best can be had for ten cents. The hyacinth bean
and scarlet runner do not make so dense a covering, but
are better than no vines. When we come to perennial
vines, the list is larger. Among those that may usually
be had without any expense, the common hop is one of
the most available. It grows wild in many places, and
is to be found in cultivation all over the country. The
common virgin's bower (*Clematis Virginiana*), the large
or hedge bindweed (*Calystegia*), often called wild morning-glory, the climbing bittersweet or wax-work (*Celas-
trus*), and Virginia creeper (*Ampelopsis*), are common,
while one or more honeysuckles are not rare. Either of
these wild plants, to be had by only the trouble of searching for and taking up, will make a dense shade, and
when the plants are well established, an abundant one.
The nearest nursery will supply at twenty-five to fifty
cents each, according to size, various fragrant honeysuckles, trumpet creeper, climbing roses, and others.
For a little more outlay the fragrant akebia, the showy
large-flowered varieties of clematis, the Dutchman's pipe,
and others may be had. We have not mentioned the
grape-vine, some varieties of which, such as the Clinton,
make a capital shade, but the temptation of the green
fruit to children make other plants more desirable.
Neither in the cost of vines, nor that of a support for

them to grow upon, need there be any good reason why any one who really wishes it, should not add the comfort of a vine to their dwelling. While those who can afford a moderate outlay will find that there is an abundance of pleasing climbers which, in the ornamental character of their foliage and fragrance and beauty of flowers, will give ample returns for the investment. We have often thought, when passing a new house, it is a pity that the cost of some of the scroll and other "ginger-bread work" on the verandas could not have been invested in vines. It is well to bear in mind that galvanized wire—about No. 14—will prove a most useful aid in carrying vines wherever they are wanted. It is desirable that vines should not run directly upon the wooden pillars of a veranda; wires may be stretched vertically about two inches from them, to which the shoots may be trained as they grow.

A SEAT IN THE GROVE.

Figure 53 shows a method of making a seat in a grove.

Fig. 53.—A BASKET YARD SEAT.

A tree had been felled, leaving a stump of convenient

hight. The top of this was made level, and surmounted with a cover of one of the modern styles of baskets, which is made of elastic splints. When this cover is attached by a strong nail in the center, it forms an inviting and convenient seat.

WHERE TO PLACE FLY SCREENS.

Take off all the springs and attachments, tie them together, and fasten each lot to its own screen; then

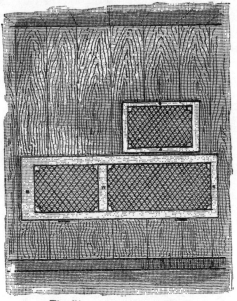

Fig. 54.—SCREENS IN WINTER.

fasten the screens with screws against the inside of some shed, as shown in figure 54. When needed, the screens may be found all together, straight and in proper condition for service, instead of being twisted, warped and broken, and their attachments scattered to the four winds, as is frequently the case with such things.

CISTERNS CHEAPLY MADE.

Every house should have a cistern. None but those who have been accustomed to the use of soft water in domestic operations, know how much superior it is to hard. It not only makes things cleaner, but the labor of cleaning is greatly lessened, while hard water ruins woollens.

The expense of building cisterns is not large. In localities where the soil is composed principally of clay, we have seen them built by digging a hole in the ground, and plastering the exposed surface with water-lime. Generally a layer of stones is placed in the bottom, over which a thin mixture of lime and water is poured. This runs down among the stones, fills all the crevices, and settles into a smooth surface above them, and, when dry, forms a floor of sufficient thickness and hardness, to allow any one to tread upon it while cleaning out the cistern, without danger of breaking the floor. Plaster the lime directly upon the slanting sides of earth, with a common trowel. Care should be taken to not mix up a great quantity at any one time, as the lime soon "sets," and it becomes impossible to smooth the walls properly, if too large a surface has been plastered over roughly, before beginning the smoothing process.

The top of the cistern should be well covered, and pains taken to see that the earth on which the wall is laid, is below frost in winter, otherwise freezing is likely to crack the coat of lime, and cleave it off, or leave cracks, through which the water will soak out. If properly banked up in winter, such a cistern will last for years; it is quite as satisfactory, indeed, as one built up of brick or stone. An opening large enough to admit a person should be left in the covering. In cleaning it, the walls can be readily washed, and all slime completely removed by using a stiff scrubbing brush. Such a cistern costs but a few dollars in its construction, and will pay for itself in a short time.

A FRUIT-DRYING ARRANGEMENT.

The usual method of drying apples, is to build a frame out of doors, cover it with boards, upon which the fruit

Fig. 55.—A FRUIT-DRYING PLATFORM.

is spread. During inclement weather, the fruit is usually only partially protected by a covering of loose boards. Figure 55 shows a good fruit-drying arrangement, located in the south side of the second story of the wood-house, corn-house, or other convenient out-building. A space eight inches high, and five or six feet in length, is cut in the south side of the building, level with the floor; upon the floor are nailed two light scantlings, *a, a,* projecting beyond the building six or eight feet, as desired. The ends are connected by the strip *h,* and supported by the braces *e, e.* Upon this track runs the platform, or drying board, *b*. The wheels may be of either wood or iron, and run in grooves, or in any way desired. When the platform is within the building, it is easy of access, and perfectly dry, and can be quickly pushed out along the track, to receive the direct rays of the sun during pleasant weather. It is up out of the way of fowls, and is so arranged that even a child can manage it, besides insuring a better quality of dried fruit, than if dried out of doors in the usual manner. The opening cut in the building should be so arranged as to be closed when the drying season is over, with a long strip of board, or, better still, arranged with hinges.

DRYING FRUIT UNDER SASHES.

Those who have hot-bed sashes can dry fruit by the heat of the sun in a manner vastly superior to the ordinary

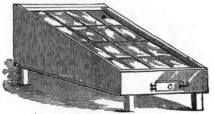

Fig. 56.—A SASH FRUIT DRIER.

method. A box should be made like a hot-bed frame, but with a bottom, and it should have legs to raise it a few inches from the ground. The sashes should fit sufficiently closely to keep out dust and insects. In the front of the box, at the bottom, make openings under the middle of each sash, and at the rear, at the top, make similar openings. These openings should be covered with wire cloth, though in its absence, mosquito netting or similar material will answer. The fruit, or other article to be dried, should be upon trays or frames covered with some coarse fabric, and raised a few inches from the bottom of the box. The sash being so placed as to catch the full heat of the sun, the drying will go on in a surprisingly rapid manner. The air passing in at the lower openings will become quickly heated, and going out at the upper openings, a current will be established, carrying off the moisture from the fruit, etc., in the most satisfactory manner. The product will not be so white as when dried by artificial heat, but for home use just as good, and it will be free from dust and the soiling by insects. We have dried the finest sweet corn imaginable with a contrivance like this, and have no doubt of its efficacy in drying fruit. An idea of the frame is given in figure 56, which shows a box with a single sash, but usually a larger drier will be required, and one arranged for three hot-bed sashes of the usual size will be none too long for ordinary use.

CHAPTER II.

THE CELLAR.

CELLARS IN GENERAL.

It would seem as though no person of good judgment would rear a house without attending first to the foundation. But this mistake is often made, especially in the West, or in new towns where there is scarcity of house-room if not scarcity of money. The house is hastily built over a kind of hole in the ground, which is to be dug out deeper and wider, and made into a cellar sometime. But work presses, and time flies, and the frame of the house settles unevenly, and water collects in the hole meant for a cellar. Sometimes years pass before the hole is made into a cellar, and sometimes this desirable change is never made—all of which is a great mistake. Better build small, and be thorough as you go on with the work. A good cellar is a very important part of a country house—a dry cellar, cool and clean in summer, frost-proof and well ventilated in winter. The cellar should extend under the whole house if possible, and be not less than seven and one-half feet deep. If the house is built on firm dry land, with sufficient slope away from the walls in all directions, there will be little difficulty in securing a dry cellar. And what if the outside covered drain, which is intended to carry away the water from the cellar, slopes inward instead of outward? This would not often happen, but we have lived over one cellar where an attempt at drainage was so unsuccessful, that we were impressed with the need of great care in that respect. There are many desirable places for a home where a dry cellar is an exception to the general rule.

(57)

But a dry cellar you must have, or suffer more or less in family health. No matter if you are poor, "Doctor's bills" cost more than sanitary measures for the preservation of health. Below is a very truthful representation of the condition of many farm-house cellars at the time of spring rains and melting snows. There is the flood in the cellar, when boxes, and barrels, and wash-tubs, and hoops, and staves are all afloat, and afterwards the horrible slime on the bottom, when the pond in the cellar has slowly oozed away, leaving behind all its poison filth. The most common method of cellar drainage—the construction of a small culvert running from a corner of the cellar to some low ground near the house, with little ditches across the cellar bottom connecting with this outlet, is quite inadequate for securing a really dry cellar. No one need imagine that a well made water-tight inside with cement, will answer as well as drainage. We know of an instance where a cellar was carefully and heavily cemented to exclude water, and the pressure of the water lifted the whole body of the cement from the bottom, leaving it in broken masses, like flag stones half on edge. It is practicable to exclude water from a cellar by a heavy wall laid in cement, and a heavy cemented floor of brick or stone, but the process is very expensive, and leaves the adjacent soil saturated with water in wet times. In vain have you sought a healthy climate for your home if your new dry and frost-proof cellar lacks some adequate means of ventilation. People become gradually accustomed to increasing cellar odors in their living-rooms and bedrooms, and breathe a tainted and unwholesome atmosphere quite unconsciously. An invalid, especially one with weak lungs, coming from a pure atmosphere into one of these cellar-tainted houses, quickly perceives the impurity of atmosphere which dwellers in the house had not observed. Perhaps this is the best mission of invalids, and no one need fear that they will ever find their occupation gone, for bad air and invalids will probably "go out" together. In building, one or more of the chimneys should be so arranged that a flue may be used for ventilating the cellar. If windows alone be depended upon, they will probably be closed and sealed by the banking outside in the coldest weather. A cellar should have both an outside and an inside entrance. It is about equally uncomfortable for a house-keeper to have all the vegetables and meat brought in through the house for winter storage, or to be obliged to run out of doors in all weathers to reach her cellar by an outside door. The cellar should be made so tight and carefully protected in every part that rats and mice can find no entrance. Drains must be protected at the outer end by copper gauze, and the windows by wire-netting in summer, so that the whole cellar may serve as a clean cool "safe" for milk and other food. A house-keeper with a good cellar, has reason to be thankful for one great comfort, and she can but show her gratitude by taking the best possible care of it, letting nothing be left there to decay, and having it well cleaned as often as the case demands, which is very thoroughly, at least every spring, boxes, barrels, and all.

MUSTY CELLAR.

A musty cellar will spoil the milk and other things in a few hours. Such a cellar wants ventilation. If ordinary ventilation by a window is not sufficient, open a communication with the chimney if possible, or place a wooden spout, eight or ten feet high, against the back or side of the house, and make the bottom of it open into the top of the cellar. Fix another tube from the outside, near the ground, which shall open at the bottom of the cellar. Thus a circulation of air will take place from the bottom to the top. Wash the cellar walls and ceiling with lime whitewash in which a little carbolic acid has been mixed; this will destroy the mould on the walls, and the ventilation will prevent its future formation.

VENTILATING A CELLAR.

To get rid of the foul air accumulating in the cellar a communication may be made between the cellar and

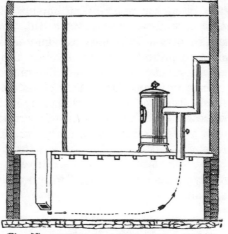

Fig. 57.—METHOD OF VENTILATING A CELLAR.

either a chimney in which there is a constant upward current of warm air, or with the pipe of the stove. A piece of stove-pipe should pass through the floor, and terminate just below it in the cellar. The end of the pipe in the room above the cellar may turn into the chimney, or if that is not practicable or desirable, it may connect with the stove-pipe. This upright pipe, which passes from the cellar, should be provided with a damper. The cellar being thus connected directly with a flue, or indirectly with it by means of the stove-pipe, in either of which is

a strong upward current, may be deprived of its foul air
in a very short time. It will not be necessary or desirable
that the ventilation be kept up continously, hence the
damper is placed in the ascending pipe. This should be
opened a short time daily, or as often as the condition of
the air in the cellar shows it to be necessary. Figure
57 will suggest the arrangement where the connection
is made with the stove. But if foul air is taken from the
cellar, it must be replaced by other air from without.
In a climate where the cold is continuously severe, it will
not answer to bring the outer air directly into the cellar,
as its contents would be frozen and spoiled. It may be
well to provide for the admission of the outer air during
mild spells, if such occur in the locality; this may be
done by making a small opening in one of the cellar windows, that may be closed by a sliding shutter. If the
air without is too cold, then the supply must be taken
from the house itself. This should be done from a point
as far distant from the exit pipe as practicable. The hall
or entry-way may be the most convenient place, but any-
where will do if the air is not too warm or too cold.

ICE BOXES OR REFRIGERATORS.

In constructing an ice-box, the first point is to exclude the warm air. To do this the box must be
double, and the space between the outer and the inner
box filled with some non-conducting material; this may
be sawdust, charcoal, dry tan-bark, or any similar substance, and this material must be kept dry. The
chief difficulty in making a home-made refrigerator is
in getting the inner box water-tight. It should be
lined with metal; zinc is the best. The size of the inner
box having been fixed upon, make an outer box about

four inches larger each way. The inner box should
have in the bottom an opening an inch in diameter,
and to the metal lining should be soldered a small
tube of the same material, six inches long, to carry off
the drip from the melted ice. Two pieces of scantling
should be placed on the bottom of the outer box, to hold
the weight of the inner one, and prevent it from pressing
upon the sawdust or other filling. A piece of coarse
sponge placed in the tube at the bottom of the inner box,
will allow the water to pass out, and prevent the warm

Fig. 58.—A HOME-MADE REFRIGERATOR.

air from entering. There should, of course, be ledges
soldered at convenient places to the zinc lining, to allow
of light wooden racks being placed here and there, to
hold the food and other articles. The best refrigerators,
arranged for the most economical use of ice, have a place
for the ice at the top, but in a home-made affair, the ice
may be placed in a large piece at the bottom. In using
an ice-chest, care must be taken to introduce no articles
that by their strong odor will injure butter, cream, or
milk, if these are placed within it. Fish and meats will
give an unpleasant flavor to butter. Where ice is plenty,
a temporary refrigerator for such strong-smelling articles

can be made by the use of a box or barrel, placing in it a lump of ice wrapped in a piece of carpet or a blanket, and setting in the articles by its side.

The materials for the refrigerator shown in figure 59 are simply two packing boxes, one of which is smaller than the other, a quantity of powdered charcoal, and a few square feet of hair-felt, such as is used for covering

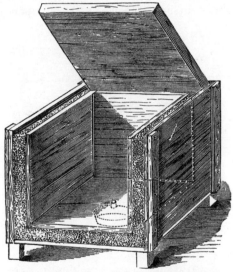

Fig. 59.—SECTION OF HOME-MADE ICE-BOX.

boilers as a non-conductor of heat, or of common oil-cloth. The engraving shows the boxes with the front parts taken away, so that the manner of placing them together may be seen. A few inches (not less than four) in depth of the powdered charcoal is laid on the bottom of the outer box, which should be lined with the felt. Then the inner box, covered on the outside with felt, is placed in the outer box. The space around it is packed tightly with the charcoal up to the top. A strip of tin

is nailed so as to cover the charcoal between the boxes.
The inner box should be lined with sheet zinc or galvanized iron. A hole is bored through the bottom, and a
short piece of lead-pipe is fixed to carry off the water
from the melted ice. The covers of the boxes are fitted
so as to have an air space between them, and felt is tacked
on to these to help keep out the heat. Common oil-cloth
will answer in place of the felt, if that can not be procured. When in use, the ice is placed upon a small

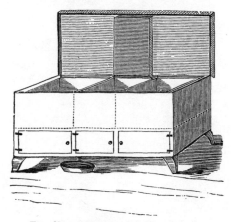

Fig. 60.—HOME-MADE REFRIGERATOR.

wooden rack with short legs, which raise it an inch or
more above the bottom of the box. The ice may be
wrapped in a piece of blanket, which will make it last
much longer than without it. If needed some rack
shelves may be fitted around the box, upon which to place
whatever is to be kept cool. The box is set upon four
short legs, or blocks, and a pan is kept beneath it to receive the waste water.

The refrigerator shown in figure 60 is a wooden box of
suitable size, having a recessed lid. It may be divided
into chambers if desired, to keep various articles separ-

ately, as butter from vegetables, or meat from fruit or pies. A central chamber with a separate lid is made in the upper part of the box to receive the ice. This should be made of sheet-zinc, and have a pipe in the bottom to permit the water to drain away as the ice melts. The shelves which divide the upper and lower parts of the box should be placed where the dotted line is shown in the cut, and should be made of slats, and movable, so that the cool air will circulate all around, and that they may be taken out to be cleaned occasionally. The box needs lining to retain the coldness communicated by the

Fig. 61.—CHEAP REFRIGERATOR.

ice. This lining should be a good non-conductor of heat, and as good a one as any is thick woollen felt, of which two thicknesses may be used, tacked on to the inside of the box, and covered with sheet-zinc soldered closely at the corners. Where the felt can not easily be procured, double walls may be made, and the space between them filled with pounded charcoal. The box should set on four feet, so that it is not in contact with the ground, and allow the water to drain off.

A box, figure 61, large enough to hold a bucket and have room around it for various dishes, pans, and jars, is made water and air-tight by covering the cracks with strips of tin and stopping them with putty inside. Insert a stop-cock at one side at the bottom, and set the

box on four blocks to raise it four or five inches from the
cellar floor. Cover the box with a tight-fitting lid. Make
a few gimlet holes in the bottom of the bucket for the
water to run out, and set it on two bricks. Wrap the
ice closely in carpet or blanket or other woollen, and put
it in the bucket. As it melts the water runs in the box
and is drawn off when necessary. Pans of milk, butter,
and any other articles of food can be set on the ice or
around the bucket. Bricks under pans keep them out of
the water, but jars and crocks may set on the bottom of
the box. Hooks in the side of the box serve for hanging
up fowls, etc. Ice in this way can be kept a long time,
especially if the box stands in the cellar.

PRESERVING SMALL QUANTITIES OF ICE.

To keep ice, it must be covered with some non-conducting material that will prevent heat from reaching it.

Fig. 62.—SECTION OF PRESERVER.

Wrapping the lump in flannel or other woollen cloth,
answers a good purpose until the covering becomes wet,
when the ice melts very rapidly. The more perfect a
non-conductor the material that surrounds the ice, and
more completely warm air is excluded, the better it will
keep. Ice has been kept an astonishing length of time

by placing it between two feather pillows, a plan that may do in an emergency, but neither convenient or desirable. Figures 62 to 64 show a preserver which can be readily made, and does good service. Figure 62 shows

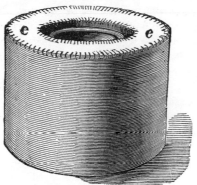

Fig. 63.—PRESERVER FOR ICE.

the affair in sections ; it consists of an outer box of pasteboard eighteen inches in diameter, and the same in hight; within this stands a cylinder of pasteboard, *b, b,* ten inches in diameter; the space between the two is filled

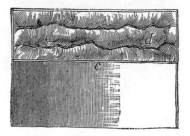

Fig. 64.—SECTION OF COVER.

with cotton batting, *d, d ;* the batting is also placed in the bottom of the cylinder to the depth of three inches, and a pasteboard cover, *c,* crowded tightly down upon it. The ice is placed in a stone jar, *F,* which stands in a saucer to catch the drip.   A circular rim of pasteboard, *e, e,* figure 63, which shows the exterior of the affair, is sewed to the outer box and inner cylinder.   The cover, which is made on the same principle, is shown in section in figure 64 ; it is of pasteboard, like the box, and has three inches of its upper part filled with batting, which is held in place by a circle of pasteboard, *c.*   When the cover is placed upon the box, the ice is surrounded on all sides by about three inches in thickness of cotton-batting, which is such a complete non-conductor that ice may be preserved in this manner for twenty-four to thirty-six hours.   A strong darning-needle, with a cork for a handle, makes a convenient pick for breaking off small pieces of ice as they are required.   The same contrivance will be found useful for keeping drinks and other matters warm; these, if set in the cylinder in place of the ice-jar, will retain their heat without much loss for several hours.

A MEAT-SAFE.

A meat-safe may be constructed by making a frame of

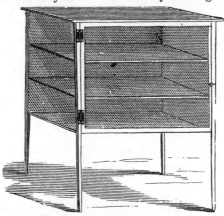

Fig. 65.—HOME-MADE MEAT-SAFE.

four upright pieces, with a close top, back, and bottom,

and two or three shelves, with a frame door at front. Mosquito-net or wire-gauze may be nailed over the frame and door, and the articles kept in the safe will thus have plenty of air, but will be kept free from flies.   On no account should any gauze be put on the top, as flies would drop their eggs through it.   Figure 65 shows a safe of this kind.

FILTER FOR WATER.

A very readily made filter for home use may be constructed in a few minutes, with very easily procured

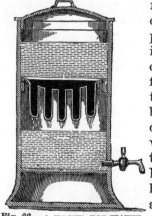

materials.   There is first needed a tin pail, divided into two parts, the upper one slipping into the other.   The upper one contains the water to be filtered.   Near the bottom of this is fixed a peculiar shaped bag, made of stout cotton cloth, doubled if need be, to prevent the charcoal from passing through with the water.   This bag is very shallow at the top, but has several long pockets, as shown in figure 66.   These

Fig. 66.—A FILTER FOR WATER.

are filled with charcoal, both fine and coarse, and the top of the bag is also covered with a layer about an inch thick.   There is a cover made to the bag, which stretches across the pail, above the upper layer of charcoal.   The bag should be fitted very tightly to the sides of the pail, and an elastic hoop may be used to thus firmly secure it.   When water is poured into the upper pail, it filters through the charcoal, and is rendered free from many unseen impurities. There are many districts in which during summer water is scarce and of inferior quality. In such places no water should be drank, unless it is first filtered or boiled. Impure water is perhaps the most prolific source of those diseases, known as summer complaints, and is most dangerous when the hot weather favors the growth of vegetable and animal bodies, too minute to be seen without a microscope.

CONVENIENCES FOR WEIGHING SMALL ARTICLES.

Those who use a spring-scale, or steelyard, for weighing butter, cheese, fruits, etc., will find a great convenience in a wooden bar or arm, like the one shown in figures 67 and

Fig. 67.—BAR IN POSITION.

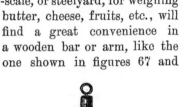

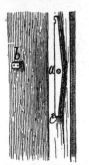

Fig. 68.—BAR THROWN UP.   Fig. 69.—METHOD OF WEIGHING A BOWL.

68. The best place for such an arm, as to light, etc., may be where a stationary bar would be greatly in the way.

Let the bar be fastened to a post by a large screw, as shown at *a*, in figure 67. When not in use, it can be thrown up in the position shown in figure 68, when it is entierly out of the way. A peg or a brad, *c*, fitting into the lower side of the block, *b*, adds security. Figure 69 shows a device for holding the butter bowl while being weighed. Three strips of wood, each two feet long, one and a half inch wide, and one inch thick, are notched to fit securely under the rim of the bowl. A loop of strong cord is tied into a hole in the upper end of each strip. The three loops are brought together and bound with twine, above which they act as a single loop for the insertion of the hook of the spring-balance.

COVER TO A PORK BARREL.

In families where pork is largely used, to cook or in cooking, the barrel, usually kept in the cellar, is frequent-

Fig. 70.—COVER CLOSED.   Fig. 71.—COVER OPEN.

ly visited, the required slices of pork cut off, and the piece returned to the brine. It is a very simple matter, but very often there is no place at hand, clean enough, or suitable, whereon to place the piece of pork, while cutting. A cover to the barrel which will make the work cleanly and easy, is shown in figure 70. The board, *A*, covers a part of the top of the barrel, being fastened by

screws, and extends over to form a shelf, surported by
the brace *E.* The remainder of the cover, *B,* is hinged
to this stationary part. When the cover is opened, as in
figure 71, it rests upon the shelf, and affords a firm, clean,
and convenient surface on which to do the cutting, and
there is no trouble in looking about for a suitable place.
These small things cost only a little time, but help
greatly to make house-work go on smoothly.

A MILK CUPBOARD.

The cupboard, figure 72, is put together with screws, so
as to be easily taken down
and packed away in sum-
mer, or when not in use,
thus occupying very little
room. The side pieces,
A, A, are inch boards six
feet long and one foot
wide. The top piece is
three and two thirds feet
long, and projects over an
inch on each side. There
are screws at *D, D,* upon
which to hang the curtain
to keep out dust and ex-
cess of heat. The slats,
B, B, upon which the
milk pans rest, are two and
one fourth inches wide,
and they are placed in
pairs four and a half inches apart, to make a shelf.

Fig. 72.—A HOME-MADE MILK
CUPBOARD.

The cleats, *O,* upon which the slats rest, have small pieces
nailed upon them, which fit into notches made in the

ends of the slats, to keep the latter from moving. The brace for the back, *C*, is let into the sides flush, as shown at *J*. The bottom shelf is solid and let into the sides, as shown. The whole cupboard, thus constructed, should be whitewashed so as to keep the odor of the wood from affecting the milk.

A HOME-MADE CHEESE PRESS.

Many farmers, especially those in the newer parts of the country, are forced by circumstances to make, with their

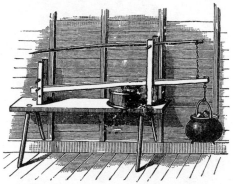

Fig. 73.—A HOME-MADE CHEESE PRESS.

own hands, many of the implements used in the house and upon the farm. Figure 73 shows a convenient and easily made cheese press, and one that has done good service for years in a household having the reputation of making the best cheese in the county. The construction of the press is simple and easily understood from the engraving. The press may stand in the middle of the room, and be worked from either side; but it will save space to have it stand against the wall. If there is a sill along the side, the legs next to the wall may be made shorter than the outside ones, and stand upon the sill. As the lever is

4

brought down, and the kettle of stones raised, it can be held in place by putting its small end under one of the pegs shown on the short standards. A woman can handle this press.

BUTTER MOLDS AND STAMPS.

Figures 74 and 75 show the usual forms of butter molds. They are made of soft wood, as white-ash or soft maple. The manner of using them is as follows: When

Fig. 74.—BUTTER-STAMP.

the butter is ready for making up, it is weighed out into the proper quantities, and each piece is worked in the butter-dish with the ladle into flat round cakes.   These cakes are either pressed with the mold shown in figure 74, or made to go into the cup of the mold shown at figure 75.   Inside of the cup (figure 75) is a mold with a handle which works through a hole in the upper part of the cup.   The cup is inverted on the table, and when this handle is pressed down it forces the mold on to the butter, which is squeezed into a very neat ornamented cake. By pushing the handle and lifting the cup, the cake of butter is pushed out of the mold. This makes a very favorite mode of putting up fine butter for market, and is also well adapted for preparing butter for the table in houses where neatness of appearances is studied. The

Fig. 75.—BUTTER-MOLD.

molds when in use should be kept wet in cold water to prevent the butter from sticking.

CONVENIENT CELLAR WINDOW.—COOL ROOM.

In a north cellar window of ordinary size, a frame is made so that the sill, top, and side casings, are over a foot wide, as they project a little in the cellar. The sash is fitted on the inside. It has three panes of glass, swings open on hinges from one side; and is securely fastened by a bolt at the other. Outside, a very heavy wire screen is tacked at the edges of the casing. We thus have a cool box of the size of the window and a foot deep. The sides and top of this frame are furnished with nails and hooks. In summer it is a very convenient place for keeping fruit, vegetables, etc., over night; in spring and autumn it serves as a refrigerator, and in the winter it is fully as useful for meat and poul-

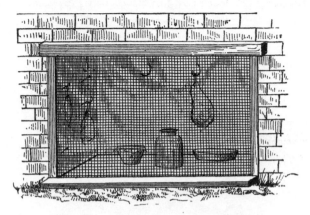

Fig. 76.—A CONVENIENT CELLAR WINDOW.

try, which keep well, hung up on the hooks.   The sill is in use every day to cool pies, cooked fruit, or puddings.

A COAL BIN.

Figure 77 shows a very convenient coal bin.   The coal

Fig. 77.—A CONVENIENT COAL BIN.

is put in at the top of the bin, *a*, and is removed through a lid in the side. The coal is kept from pressing against this lid by a slanting board at *c*. The bottom of the bin, *d*, is slanting, the upper and front sides of which come even with the lower edge of the lid. The box can be made either plain or ornamented, and if the latter, it is far superior in its appearance to the unsightly coal 'scows' frequently seen.

ANOTHER COAL BIN.

A packing-box of sufficient size, cut sloping at the top, and furnished with a lid, will make an excellent coal-bin,

Fig. 78.—A CONVENIENT COAL BIN.

or it may be made of rough or dressed boards, and painted. It should be raised a few inches from the ground, by being placed upon stout posts, or a few bricks, and the top should be of such a hight that coal may be shovelled directly into it from a wagon-box. A sliding-door should be made in the front, with a small, sloping platform, from which to shovel up the coal which escapes when the door is lifted. The door should be kept closed when not in use, in order that coal may not be scattered about. If shed-room is scarce, the bin may be kept near the back door, but it is always better to have it placed, when possible, under cover. Figure 78 shows the shape and proportions of a very convenient coal-bin. If wood or coal can not be reached without going out of doors, then the kitchen should be provided with a coal or wood box, as the case may be, and it should be made the especial business of some one, to see every morning that it contains a full day's supply.

A SMALL COAL BOX.

The accompanying section (figure 79), is from front to rear. The lower part of the box is fifteen by twenty-six inches, and sits upon a base three inches high. The whole hight of the box is twenty-six inches, and the narrower, upper portion, is fifteen inches square. Within is a sloping partition d, which divides the interior into two compartments, one for the coal, and the other, to which there is access by a door at h, holds kindlings and paper. At the top there is a lid, g, which opens as shown at a. At e is a

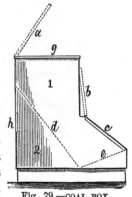

Fig. 79.—COAL BOX.

slanting board, upon which the coal is shovelled up; above this is the sloping lid, c, which opens upward as at b. If the lid, g, is covered with zinc, it makes a very convenient place upon which to set hot articles.

CHAPTER III.

THE KITCHEN.

IMPROVE THE KITCHENS.

In these days of beauty and artistic effect in houses, we are constantly told how to decorate our drawing-rooms and bedrooms, but seldom do we hear anything said about improving our kitchens. Some kitchens we have seen, especially those which were presided over by the lady of the house, were neatness itself, (this always has a charm,) but which, with a little contrivance and very little outlay, might gain in attractiveness. In a kitchen, where there is not much money to spend for adornment, let a little forethought and as much taste as possible have their way, and the owners thereof will be astonished to see how much comfort tired mother and father would take in the transformed apartment, as they drop down there for a few moment to rest.

The problem is, what shall be done to the kitchen to make it bright and attractive, and the suggestions given are intended particularly for country kitchens, which seem to be very often the thoroughfare, if not the resting-place for the family. Vines, of course, would be in the way in the summer, and at that time they are not needed so much, as the kitchen doors are frequently draped with honeysuckles or morning-glories on the outside, as well as the kitchen windows. But in the winter, when it is cold and cheerless outside, and the graceful vines have turned into brown, dead-looking stalks, try to have something green and fresh in the kitchen. Train a vine, if only a sweet-potato vine, on one of the windows, and besides, having saved all the empty cans from canned fruit or vegetables, paint a couple of them red; have two holes bored in each near the top, for the strings to pass through, by which they are to be suspended over the window. In one plant "wandering Jew," or a tradescantia, so easy to grow from slips, and which will soon run on the sides, making it a thing of beauty; and in the other hanging can, nearly full of water, lay an old sponge or piece of white cotton, over which sprinkle flax seeds thickly, keeping the cotton moist where they are sown. In two or three weeks these will sprout, and the cotton will be covered with a beautiful green mossy looking growth.

Save the old kitchen chairs; cut off the broken backs close to the seats, also the lower part of the legs, to make them of a convenient and comfortable hight. Then make a bag the size of the seat, of some old ticking or other material, and stuff it with fine shavings or slivered husks, and after nailing it securely on the seats, cover with bright cretonne or chintz. The former can be bought for twenty or twenty-five cents a yard, and would be forwarded from a city store on sending the order, and giving an idea of the ground color wanted. Two or three palm leaf fans tastily painted would decorate the wall very prettily. If the edges are worn, they can be bound with some handsome material. The lower part of the dresser would look well, if, instead of being covered with the usual pieces of scalloped newspapers, it were covered with a strip of crash towelling, the ends fringed out, and hanging down about a quarter of a yard or so, and the center ornamented tastily with a large letter in red cotton or worsted embroidery.

These hints are simple, but they are only given for the benefit of those tired-out people, who have little time to think of improvements themselves, but who, when they once begin to act on the suggestions of others, will often find it comparatively easy to improve the appearance of rooms, and give even their kitchens an air of beauty.

A FLOUR-BOX.

An easily made flour-box is shown in figure 80. It can be made without the four drawers, closet, and spice

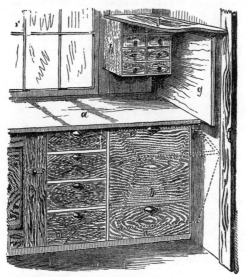

Fig. 80.—FLOUR-BOX AND ACCESSORIES.

drawers, though these are all convenient. The top, *a*, is made of one and a quarter inch pine, twenty-two inches wide. The flour-box, *b*, is sixteen inches wide inside at top, and fourteen inches at bottom; depth, fifteen inches inside; length of end boards, thirty inches; width of front, nineteen inches; length, twenty-four inches outside. These dimensions may be varied, but the ends, *c*, figure 81, should be preserved. They rest on pieces of thick leather, fastened to them and to the floor when finished. A strip, *e*, is screwed under the top, for the box to shut and open against.

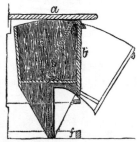

The back should be screwed on firmly. The spice drawers are made of tin, six inches by six inches, with black walnut fronts, two to three inches deep, and lettered. They set in a case m a d e o f three-eighths-inch white-wood. The molding-board, *g*, is slid behind them when not in use. The draw-

Fig. 81.—SECTION OF FLOUR-BOX.

ers, *m* and *n*, are always useful for sugar, Graham or buckwheat, towels, baking tins, and a score of things. The closet, *k*, is for syrups, lard, butter, eggs, etc. Three shelves are in the corner, though only one, *j*, is shown.

BOX FOR HOLDING SPICES.

Many steps can be saved in doing housework by having the various articles required kept together, and near at hand. A wooden box for holding spices, like the one shown in figure 82, is a most convenient little affair. It is large enough to hold ten medium-sized baking powder tin cans, holding half a pint each. A lid is fastened on with small hinges, and provided with a hook for closing. A narrow strip of leather is tacked from the inside of the lid to the inside of each end of the box, to prevent the lid from opening too far. The name of the spice con-tained is marked on the top of each can, with common white paint. The letters may first be drawn with a lead pencil, to serve as a guide for the brush. The outside of the box may be finished in any way to suit the taste, with the word "Spices," in dark-brown on the front. To make the box more ornamental, a pattern may be cut out of heavy paper, and fastened to the wood with mucilage. After the staining has been applied, and the paper taken off, the pattern will look as if inlaid. The staining should imitate walnut or some dark wood. A good design is a

Fig. 82.—A CONVENIENT SPICE-BOX.

small group of leaves in each corner. The veins and a little shading may be put on the leaves after the paper is taken off, by using a small brush and the staining liquid. A simple border may be put around the top of the box and the lid.

A FOLDING IRONING TABLE.

An ironing table should be abundantly long, and for the use of most persons, six inches higher than the common dining or kitchen table. The surface of many tables, when used for ironing, is sadly disfigured by the hot iron, which blisters and dissolves the varnish. A very cheap and extremely convenient ironing table is shown in figure 83; it is made by securing to the wainscoting, or directly to the wall, with hinges, the board, *B*, which is three and one-half feet wide, and five or six feet in length. The board is here shown folded down, entirely out of the way. The manner of folding and

Fig. 83.—IRONING TABLE FOLDED.

securing the legs, is seen in figure 84. One leg is hinged at each outer corner of the board, and when folded, one end of the clasp, P, is turned over them, as shown, keep-

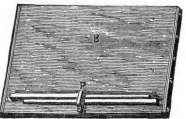

Fig. 84.—UNDERSIDE OF BOARD.

ing them from sagging, and always in place when the board is not in use. The table is easily secured to the wall of any room, and could be used in a well ventilated shed or summer kitchen in summer, and in the regular kitchen in winter.

A CONVENIENT SIDE TABLE.

Figure 85 shows two side shelves or tables, one folded down and the other raised ready for use. The "leaf" or top is first hung by hinges to a back strip fastened upon the wall with large screws. The front of the leaf, when

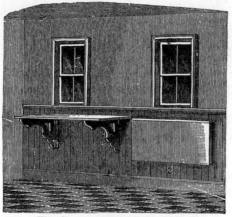

Fig. 85.—A FOLDING SIDE TABLE.

raised, is supported by brackets which are fastened to the wall by hinges or butts. When swung in against the wall, as indicated by dotted lines, (1) the leaf falls down and is out of the way, as shown at 2 in the engraving. There are but few dining-rooms or kitchens where one or more such folding side tables would not be useful, while the cost is but trifling.

BOX FOR HOLDING SCOURING MATERIALS.

A box in which all the various materials required for burnishing silverware, knives, brass, and the more com-

mon tinware may be kept, is a convenience to every
house-keeper. A very useful box for the purpose is easily
made from a small wooden one, by placing a few parti-
tions in it, and a drawer in the lower part. The one
shown in figure 86 was made from a starch-box, and the
wooden boards used to form the divisions, are fastened in
place with screws. The lower portion of the front is cut
out, and a drawer fitted in. This drawer has a strip ten
inches deep across the front, but none around the sides
or back. It readily slips in and out, and can be entirely
removed when knives are scoured upon it. The upper
part is divided into three compartments, the largest for
holding the soft cloths and brushes used for scouring, the

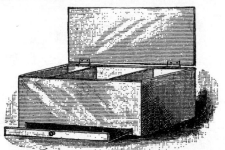

Fig. 86.—A CONVENIENT SCOURING BOX.

next largest for the bath-brick, scouring soaps and sand,
used for knives and general scouring purposes, and the
smallest for the finer powders used on silverware. The
drawer has a small knob on the front. The lid is fastened
on by suitable hinges.

A medium-sized cork is much better than a cloth for
scouring knives, and if the bath-brick is pulverized and
put in a bottle, it is always ready for use. Nothing but
the finest of powder should be used on silver. Bath-brick
should never be employed, as the coarse grains scratch
and mar the silver. Before scouring, the silver should be
well washed in hot water, to which one teaspoonful of

liquid ammonia to one quart of water has been added. It should never be washed in soap suds, for the soap will soon give it a dull appearance. Silver can be made bright by the use of prepared chalk (whiting), mixed into a paste with ammonia. It should be mixed as wanted. A good scouring soap is made by cutting a one-pound bar of laundry soap into small pieces, and dissolving it in hot water, using as little water as possible. After being dissolved, stir into it enough fine river sand to make it thick, then spread on a shelf to dry. Cut into cakes, and let it dry well before using. The longer it stands before using, the better, and it is a good plan to make a quantity at a time. Ammonia, bath-brick powder, and kerosene mixed together, are good for cleaning zinc and brass.

A BREAD OR KNEADING BOARD.

The idea is, to have a board for the bread which shall be used for that purpose only, that may be readily taken

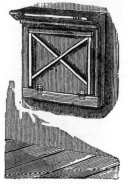

Fig. 87.—BREAD-BOARD FOLDED AGAINST WALL.

Fig. 88.—BREAD-BOARD OPEN FOR USE.

down and put away, and when not in use shall occupy but little room and at the same time be protected from dust.

Figure 87 shows the board when not in use, and figure 88 the same when ready for work. Where the wall of the kitchen is plastered, a lining (1, fig. 88) corresponding to the size of the board will be needed, but if the walls are wainscoted, this is not necessary. Above the lining is a box cornice, the front of which lifts up, and opens a place where the rolling pin, cake cutters, etc., are kept. The board (2) is three feet square and an inch and a-quarter thick, with an inch and a-half cleat securely fastened at each end, to prevent warping. No wood so suitable for the board itself as soft maple, but all the other parts may be of pine. ' The board is hinged to a strip (3) of the same thickness, and provided with light legs (4), to support it at a convenient hight when down; these are hinged to the board, and drop down, as in figure 87, when that is not in use.

A CONVENIENT BAKING TABLE.

The table from which figure 89 is made stands under a north window, in a large kitchen, is convenient to the

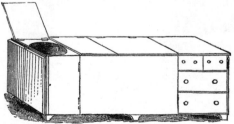

Fig. 89.—A CONVENIENT BAKING TABLE.

stove, and arranged to hold all or nearly all the articles needed in baking. The table is two and a-half feet wide, six feet long, and high enough to take in an ordinary flour barrel, from which three inches of its top has been cut. It is made perfectly tight, and is raised three inches from the floor on six feet. It has four compartments. The first is to hold the flour barrel, and beside the lid in the top, has a door in the front. The second compartment has a sliding partition in the center, and is for Indian meal and Graham flour. The third compartment has a similar partition, and holds sugar. The last compartment is fitted up with drawers for holding baking powder, soda, cream of tartar, spices, extracts, etc. The top of the table is finished for use in making bread. A board for molding bread is made to fit on the top, two and a half feet square, and when not in use, hangs at the side of the table by a ring and hook. Where baking is to be done for a large family, a table should be devoted exclusively to that purpose, and one like the illustration will be found much more convenient than an ordinary kitchen table.

A CONVENIENT WASH BENCH.

A good, strong wash bench is a household article that

Fig. 90.—A FOLDING WASH BENCH.

is always appreciated by those who have to work over it. In many cases benches are made too frail, and soon become loose in the joints, if they do not quite break down, or they do not set level and steady, and the tub is continually slipping. Figure 90, shows a wash bench which is both simple and substantial. It is made of two three by three-inch joist, about three feet in length. Cut them both in the middle, as shown in figure 91, so that they will cross like a pair of shears. The legs, one in each end of the joists, may be about twenty inches to the top of the bench. After setting the tub upon the center of the bench, mark where the outside comes on the joist, and bore holes for pegs, which, when placed in,

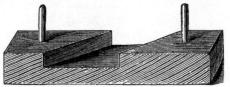

Fig. 91.—ONE OF THE BARS.

figure 91, will hold the tub firmly in place. Other holes may be bored for smaller or larger tubs. When not in use, the "shears"—which should have a bolt through the center—may be closed and the wash-bench set out of the way.

AN IMPROVED WASH BENCH.

Figure 92 shows a wash bench with a very simple attachment that will hold the clothes wringer firm and steady, and save changing it from one tub to the other. It consists of a board as long as the bench is wide, and three inches higher than a common tub, attached to the center of the bench by curved cleats, *e, e,* as shown in the engraving. At the top near the center is driven a piece of wire projecting upward about two inches. A light board, *b,* is hung upon this wire. The wringer is attached to the upper side of the board, *a*, and upon either side of board *b*. It is seen that with the wringer in position, clothes may be run from the tub to either

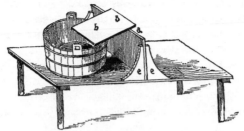

Fig. 92.—IMPROVED WASH BENCH.

end of the bench. This arrangement is particularly adapted to those who use a wash board, or a washing machine, placed within the tub.

EASY WASHING OF CLOTHES.

There is not much difference in the various kinds of good soap now in the market. A little common sense or scientific understanding is better than a "magic" quality in the soap. In reading the directions on the wrappers, one sees that the manufacturers mean to make us use plenty of their soap. They unite in advising that the clothes be soaked in strong, warm suds a little while— from twenty minutes to an hour—before rubbing. This process, with any good, clean soap, will make the clothes free from dirt with very slight rubbing. It is well to have a small quantity of water, only moderately warm, not hot, as clear hot water will set dirt and stains, and make them much harder to cleanse. Place some of the clothes in this, and when wet, rub the soap on one garment at a time, especially upon the parts most soiled. Then roll up the garment tightly, and cover it with water, and soap and roll the next piece. Place the dirtiest clothes by themselves, using several tubs, pails, and other utensils, if more convenient. Leave them all tightly rolled and soaped, under lukewarm water, for about half an hour—longer if you choose, but not over night, as some advise. Warm up the water by the addition of more hot water—the hotter the better, now that the clothes are well soaked. A warm, strong suds makes the rubbing easy, even when the washboard is used.

In employing a common, cheap, but clean soap, drop less than a level teaspoonful of powdered borax into the bottom of the tub, pouring hot water on it, and then cooling to the proper degree. This borax makes the washing more easy, and is good for the hands, healing them when chapped, and leaving them in good condition after washing. Whatever good soap you use, it is not necessary to boil the clothes, but this process helps in most cases, especially if the clothes are well stirred about in the boiler. It is not best to leave them actually boiling many minutes, as this will turn them yellow. The whole washing may be done without warm water, if desired, but more or stronger soap must be used, and the labor is harder. We want to loosen the dirt between the fibres as easily as possible, and then to rinse it all away. That is the philosophy of making soiled clothes clean.

DISH SINK WITH RACKS FOR DRAINING.

Dish washing loses many of its unpleasant features if a sink like the one shown in figure 93, is used. It is a little longer than an ordinary sink, is lined with sheet-iron instead of zinc, and is made with two divisions. The largest one is for draining the dishes and is furnished with a waste-pipe for carrying the water into a bucket placed below. If the house is supplied with water, the pipe from the sink should connect with other waste-pipes, and the bucket be dispensed with. The sink is also furnished with wooden racks for draining, which can be removed when not in use. They are frames made of thin strips of wood. The supports are put on so that by

Fig. 93.—WASH SINK FOR KITCHEN.

unfastening the hook they will fold up against the rack, and take up little room. Part of the space under the sink is inclosed and made into a small cupboard, with one large and two small drawers above, in which are to be kept dish-towels, cloths, and scouring materials.

VEGETABLE SLICER AND GRATER.

The simple contrivance, shown in figure 94, may be made by any neat carpenter, and by almost any one apt in the use of tools. It is a box, or trough, about ten inches by twenty inches, open at one end and on the top, strongly made of inch stuff, furnished with stout cleats on the sides, upon which is a smaller box, without top or bottom, which may be moved back and forth through the box. Slides, very strongly made, to bear pressure, are fitted to rest upon the same cleats, but lower down, so as not to interfere with the free motion of the box over them. These slides are either graters for horse-radish, carrots, etc., or furnished with knives for slicing cabbage, or any other vegetables so used in the household economy. In use, the article to be sliced or grated—say a cabbage head—is placed in the little box, shown in the engraving, and, the knife slide being inserted, it is moved back and forth, bearing with the hand upon it until enough is cut

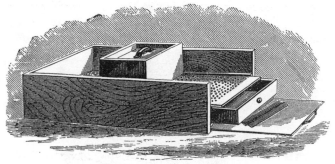

Fig. 94.—GRATER AND SLICER.

off to enable the little follower to be put in, and after this the slicing is continued until it is all cut up. A drawer beneath catches the shavings, or the gratings, and, if desirable, a place may be made to keep the slide when not in use.

A CABBAGE CUTTER.

Cabbage is usually shaved into thin strips before being cooked, and this little affair shown in figure 95, does the work quickly and well. It cuts fine enough for slaw, and can be used to slice potatoes for frying by adjusting the knives to cut the required thickness.

It consists of a board about three feet long and a foot wide. In the center of this board, fitted diagonally across a square opening, are knives, usually made out of old scythes, and set slanting like a plane-iron. To each edge of this bottom board are fitted strips having a flange on the upper part. The end-pieces of the box have notches cut in them to fit these flanges, which make a track for the box to slide on. It is best to make the strips of hard-wood. The box is slipped in on these flanges, and the cabbage, or whatever is to be cut, is placed in the box and snugly pressed down. By sliding the box back and forth, and keeping the contents pressed down, each push shaves off a

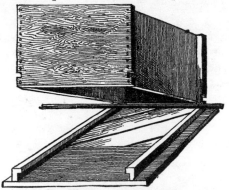

Fig. 95.—A CABBAGE CUTTER.

thickness, precisely as a plane takes off shavings from a board. These shavings fall through the openings between the knives, and drop into the pan or tub over which the apparatus is placed. Small cutters for the same use, with but a single knife and without the box, are sold at the house-furnishing stores, under the name of "vegetable slicers."

A HOME-MADE BUTTER WORKER.

The butter-worker shown in figure 96, has been in use for years, and is liked very much. The sink is in a little unfinished room, and has a bench adjoining it. About midway of this bench is a joist. A small square

piece of board is nailed to the lower part of this joist
next to the bench, so that one side projects two and a
half inches.   A round hole, an inch above the bench,
in the corner of the square piece, serves as a socket
for the end of the "butter-worker."   A little knob,
nailed to the bench, acts as a rest for the worker-
board, and allows the hand under the edge of the
board, to turn it around as the butter is being worked.
The edge opposite the hand rests on the bench.   The
person using it grasps the worker in the right hand,
and turns the board, to bring the butter in the right
position, with the left hand.

The board is made of maple, and is fourteen inches
in diameter, and three-fourths inch thick.   The worker

Fig. 96.—A HOME-MADE BUTTER WORKER.

was made from an old ash-wagon thill, and is thirty-
two inches long, two and one-fourth inches wide, and
three-fourths inch thick.   One edge is bevelled down
almost sharp, and the other is round.   A little groove
should be made in the bench to allow the buttermilk
to run off into a dish.   Wet both board and worker

thoroughly outside with pure water previous to using, to prevent the butter from sticking.

A COOKING STEAM PIPE.

The unpleasant odor that pervades the house while cabbage is being cooked may be avoided by fitting a tube to the lid of the pot or boiler, which conveys the steam from the cooking cabbage into the pipe of the stove, as shown in figure 97. A tinsmith, if told to make

Fig. 97.—A COOKING STEAM-PIPE.

such a tube to carry off the steam from the cooking-pot to the stove-pipe would have the tube shut on over, or on the outside of the socket placed on the pot-lid. It should be inserted on the inside of the socket. Some of the steam will be condensed in the tube, and the water will run back. If the pipe shuts over the socket this water would drip upon the hot stove, and increase the trouble; placing it within the socket, it falls back into the pot.

5

DON'T SPOIL THE MEATS.

Any flesh heated sufficiently, will, just like wood, be reduced to charcoal (carbon) and water, and a little gaseous matter.   The water and gas escape into the atmosphere, the charcoal will remain, unless heated sufficiently in the open air to form carbonic acid gas, when that will also go off, leaving only a little ashes.   Well, in roasting, baking, grilling or broiling, and frying meats of all kinds, every minute's continuation of heat beyond just enough to coagulate the albumen, does something towards changing the meat into charcoal, and charcoal is innutritious and indigestible.   Further, rare cooked, fresh, lean beef, will digest and go into nourishment in two to three hours, while "well done" beef, and well corned beef need four to four and a half or five hours to digest in strong stomachs, and longer in feeble ones.   Nine-tenths or more of families cook meats too much, for health, for good digestion, and for getting the best nourishment from them. It is a matter of habit.   Rare cooked meats, "blood rare" —that is, only barely well heated through—are far more digestible and nutritious, and when one "breaks himself into" the habit of eating them rare, they will be more toothsome than if "well done."   These are facts; act in accordance with them.

A CLOTHES DRIER.

The clothes drier shown in figure 98, gives a large amount of hanging room for the space it occupies.   It is made of light stuff, with the exception of the two standards and the foot pieces, which should be of hardwood.   The construction of this drier is so plain, from the engraving, that no description need be given.

Any one at all apt with tools can make this useful
household convenience. When not in use the parts

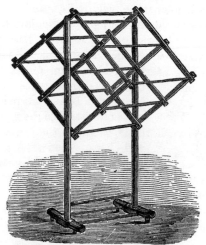

Fig. 98.—A CONVENIENT CLOTHES RACK.

can be folded together, and the drier will then occupy
but a very little space.

Figure 99 shows a perspective view of an unpatented
clothes-horse, which is five feet long and four and a half

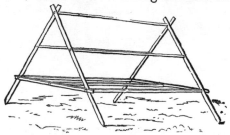

Fig. 99.—CLOTHES-HORSE EXTENDED.

feet high. It requires in its construction neither nails
nor screws, the whole being fastened together by wooden
pins through the ends of the bars, which project through

holes in the uprights. The bars are one inch square, but rounded at the ends to go through the uprights, which are three-fourths inch by two inches. The end view is given in figure 100; perpendicular dotted lines

Fig. 100.—END VIEW.

show the manner in which the clothes hang, and it will be seen that those upon one bar will not come in contact with those upon another. The cross-pieces at the ends are attached by one of their ends to one of the horizontal bars, and hook upon another bar by means of a notch near the opposite end. By unhooking the cross-pieces, as shown by the dotted lines, and removing the lower center bar, the horse can be folded up and occupy but a small space.

Figure 101 shows a clothes-horse when opened. When it is not in use, it can be folded so that it takes up

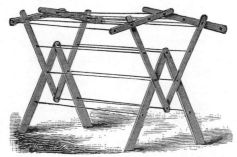

Fig. 101.—A CONVENIENT HOME-MADE CLOTHES-HORSE.

only a few inches of space, and can therefore be easily placed out of the way. The size of the "bars" will depend upon the requirements of the family.

A CLOTHES-RACK.

Figures 102 to 106 show a rack for drying small articles, that is easily made and very convenient. The back can be formed to suit the fancy, and made of whatever wood

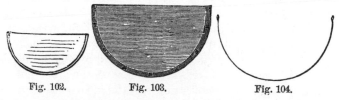

Fig. 102.   Fig. 103.   Fig. 104.

may be preferred; if of pine or bass-wood, it may be stained. The upper shelf or rest (figure 102) for the rods is a semi-circle fastened by screws inserted at the back. It

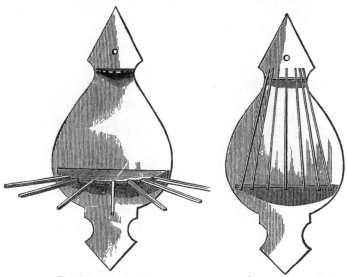

Fig. 105.—RACK OPEN.   Fig. 106.—RACK CLOSED.

need not be more than one-half-inch in thickness. The lower shelf (figure 103) should be at least an inch and a half thick, and is a semi-circle, the diameter of which is two inches less than the width of the back upon which it is to be fastened.   In the rim of this shelf cut a groove sufficiently deep to allow the wire (figure 104) to be sunken to the depth of one-fourth inch.   The wire being bent in circular form, passes through the rods or slats, which should be three-eighths inch in thickness, at the fastened end, figure 105.   The ends having a thread cut upon them, and passing through the back are fastened by small nuts. It will be seen that the rods are bevelled at the lower end, and a corresponding bevel, three-eighths inch wide, must also be cut on the under edge of the lower shelf at intervals, the number of bevels corresponding to the number of rods required.   The rods when in use should be as nearly level as possible, as shown in figure 105.   When not in use, they are merely turned up against the upper rest or shelf, as seen in figure 106.

AN IRON POT SCRUBBER.

The cleaning of pots and pans is a work that housekeepers would gladly avoid if they

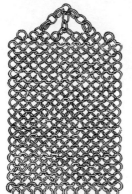

could.   Pots must be cleaned, however, and to save the finger nails, chips, spoons, knives, and other substitutes are used.   In some parts of the country, a potscrubber made of iron rings, as shown in figure 107, is used, but it is by no means so well known as it ought to be, as it serves a most excellent purpose.   It is shown as it appears when spread out; but when taken in the hand may

Fig. 107. WIRE DISH-WASHER. be gathered up in the same manner as a piece of cloth.   When anything sticks to the pot or other utensil, or has been burned to the bottom of it, a little hard rubbing with this scrubber quickly removes it; and when the pot merely needs rinsing, the scrubber may be loosely rubbed around a few times.

REMOVING FRUIT STAINS.

Fruit stains are not difficult to remove if one precaution is observed : all attempts to take out the stains should be made before the article is washed. Soap, in many cases, fixes the stain, making it much more difficult to remove. Many stains are discharged simply by the use of boiling water. Let one person hold the article a little stretched, another pours boiling water upon the spot. Burning a common sulphur match beneath a stain will often cause it to disappear at once, but the spot must be wet, else the sulphur fumes will not act. The most convenient application for fruit stains of all kinds is " Javelle Water," a solution of chlorinated potash sold at the drug shops. A solution of " Bleaching Powder" (the so-called chloride of lime), is sometimes recommended. It will take out the stains, but the combination of the lime with soap, when the article is washed, will make the fabric harsh and unpleasant. The javelle water is similar in composition, potash being used in place of lime. When javelle water is used, dip the stained portion first in hot water, then wet it with the javelle, and rinse at once. The javelle water is often much stronger than need be, and experiment will show how much it may be diluted, and still remove the stain. The application should be made just before the articles go into the wash. Where the stains are upon printed or colored materials, it is likely that the colors will be destroyed by javelle water. A small piece of the material should be tested before using it. For stains on such articles boiling water should be tried first.

A SAVING OF SOAP.

The contrivance, figure 108, consists of two cups of wire gauze, each at the end of a spring handle. Left to themselves these cups spring apart by the elasticity of the handle, but they are brought together and held in close contact by means of a simple catch. In the use of soap, the pieces become, after a while, too small to be

Fig. 108.—SOAP SHAKER.

convenient. This affair is intended to hold the small bits of soap, which are put in the cage formed by the two cups. The handle allows the soap to be used in the water for washing dishes or for other purposes. By shaking the cage in the water the soap is utilized to the last fragment.

A KITCHEN PRESS.

The ordinary method of extracting juice from fruits, lard from scraps, and the like, is by placing the mate-

Fig. 109.—A KITCHEN PRESS.

rial in a strong cloth and wringing and twisting by the main strength of the hands and arms. Screw presses serve a much better purpose, but are more or less expensive. Much aid may be derived from the use of a simple lever press, made upon the principle of a lemon squeezer, shown in figure 109. The halves are made of oak or other hard-wood, two feet long, three inches wide, and three-fourths inch thick. These are shaped at one end into handles, and hinged at the other. It requires two persons to manage this; one to hold the material in

Fig. 110.—PRESS ON TABLE.

the bag or cloth, and the other to apply the pressure. Figure 110 shows how the same press may be arranged to be worked by one person ; one of the halves of the press is hinged to a piece of board two feet long and fourteen inches wide, and set upon a table with one end elevated in the manner represented in figure 110.

A DRINK FOR THE HARVEST FIELD.

One who travels in the sparsely settled portions of Northern Mexico, is quite sure to make the acquaintance of pinole (pronounced pee-no-lee). Those who go on long journeys on horseback, and herders of cattle, who may be weeks absent from their homes, are sure to have a supply of pinole. It forms one of the principal rations of the Mexican soldiers on the frontier. Having often found pinole most acceptable on a long journey, we know it would be an excellent thing in the harvest field, or wherever a refreshing drink was required by those who need food rather than stimulants. It is often advised to use in the harvest field oat-meal stirred in water, and this is no doubt good, but pinole is better. But let us state what pinole is. Indian corn is parched, not popped, but thoroughly roasted quite through, and in doing this it should be carefully stirred, so that it will become equally and but slightly browned. This is then ground about as fine as Indian-meal, and mixed with sufficient sugar to suit the taste. It is usually flavored with cinnamon or other spices. When a tablespoonful of this pinole is stirred in a cup of cold water, it is not only acceptable to the taste, but is really nutritious, and one can travel for a long time upon this alone. The corn is thoroughly cooked, and is as useful a food as if made into bread. It is usually employed in this manner as a drink, but we have known it to be merely moistened, to make a sort of pudding, and eaten in that manner. One of the finest exhibitions of hospitality we ever met with was on the Mexican frontier. Seeing a cattle-herder's hut, we rode up to inquire the way ; the occupants of the hut, an old man and his old wife, were at dinner. They were squatted on the ground floor of the hut ; their table service consisted solely of a gourd shell, in which some pinole had been moistened, to make a sort of hasty pudding. There were no spoons, but they made use of their fingers, making alternate "grabs" at the moistened pinole, and conveying it to their mouths. This was their whole meal, as it had been for several days, yet the heartiness with which we were asked to dismount and partake of the best they had, was most charming, and made an impression that many years has not removed. The experiment with pinole can easily be tried. Corn should be slowly and carefully parched ; it may then be ground in a clean coffee-mill, if no other mill is at hand. We do not know the proportion of sugar, but that may be easily learned by experiment, and the same may be said of the spices. Pinole has the advantage over oatmeal used in making a drink, in the fact that it is thoroughly cooked and the more readily digestible.

A BOX FOR KNIVES AND FORKS.

A knife box is not a new thing, and in giving an engraving of one, we do it to remind those who are still without this useful article,—of its great utility. A knife box should be large enough to hold the knives and forks in every day use, and nothing more. It should be so

Fig. 111.—KNIFE BOX.

constructed, as to not be ugly; in fact, it ought to be neat, and of a shape to take up no extra room in the pantry. The handle should be large and sensible, and the partition through the middle of the box always separate the knives from the forks; there should be a lid to each side, to keep out the dust, as in figure 111.

FRAME FOR COOLING PIES, CAKES, ETC.

Every house-keeper knows the consequence of letting pies, tarts, or cake stand on a solid surface while cooling. The pie-crust, which should be flaky and light, becomes soggy and moist, and the bottom of the brown crusty cake soaks and loses its delicious flavor. Some kinds of fruit pies are so juicy that they have to be put on a plate when removed from the tin, but unless that renders it necessary, they should never be put on a plate until cold. The frame shown in figure 112 is made of strips of pine, three feet long and two and one half feet wide, and covered with gauze wire, such as is used for sieves. At each corner, blocks are fastened for feet, to raise the frame three inches from the table, so that

Fig. 112.—A COOLING FRAME FOR PIES AND CAKES.

the air can circulate freely beneath it. The wire is fastened to the frame by small tacks. The frame is so simple that any one apt with a hammer and saw would have no trouble in making it.

A SMALL TOASTER.

A toasting-fork is not a convenient affair to use over a stove fire, the position in which it must be held exposes the hands unpleasantly to heat, and there is danger that the slice will fall off. Figure 113 shows a small

Fig. 113.—BREAD TOASTER.

toaster. It is made of copper wire, a little larger than a common knitting needle, bent into the form shown. The broad part is five inches across each way ; the wire being bent in the form of a Maltese cross, is much firmer than a simple square or circle would be.   Below this part the ends of the wire are twisted together for about an inch, and lie side by side until they enter the handle; this straight portion is seven inches long, and fits into a wooden handle of about the same length.   There are two pieces like this—but one, to avoid confusion, being shown—set into the handle in such a manner as to spring apart an inch or more; a common curtain ring slides upon the straight portion, to bring the two halves together and hold the bread.   It takes two and a quarter yards of wire, which should be cut in halves, and the bending to form the cross should begin in the middle of each.   This toaster may be made in a very short time, and is a neat present for a boy to make his mother.

GOOD AND BAD COOKING.

House-keepers or cooks do a vast amount of mischief by the perversion of taste, and the subsequent derangement of the stomach.   Making sour bread is one of their most common sins.   Many do not know when bread is sour, and supply it with a distinctly acid flavor, believing that it is very "nice," because it is so very light.   They suppose bread is sour only when all the vinous fermentation has changed to the acetic.   Bread is sour as soon as it tastes at all sour.   This may go on increasing, but to the best bread-maker the least acid flavor is a source of grief.   Really good bread is positively sweet, and will be just as light and spongy as the nicest sour bread, if good material and proper care are used.   In families where the taste is perverted by sour bread, other abominations are usually tolerated—biscuit tasting either of excess of soda, or of bitter buttermilk; vegetables seasoned with bad butter, pie-crust strongly flavored with lard or tallow; cake tasting of rancid butter, etc.   Along with this

diet naturally goes a deal of spicing to cover the bad
flavors, or much washing down with hot, strongly seasoned coffee or tea. Sour bread is never good in milk,
and children prefer to lunch on pie or cake, rather than
on sour bread and milk or butter. The whole family
eat as little bread as possible, and the butcher's bill is
very heavy—and they call this "good living!" Just
count the empty bottles labelled "Bitters" or "Blood
Purifier," that lie around the house, where sour bread
and "good living," as generally understood, either or
both hold sway !

The plainest food can be made to taste very good
simply by selecting, preparing, and preserving it. Those
who eat food selected and prepared with chief reference
to its nourishing qualities, eating moderately to gratify a
natural appetite, instead of a morbid craving, really
enjoy eating more than the gormand or glutton, whose
chief pleasure is in eating, and who must have everything fixed up "good," with condiments or hot sauces,
and washed down with stimulants. He becomes inca-
pable of detecting and appreciating delicate flavors, and
so wears out the sense of taste, that it is hard work to
find anything that he can relish ; while a dish of good
bread and good unskimmed milk, seems very delicious to
people with undepraved appetites. Recently we heard a
little girl who does not like bread and milk, say of a
piece of bread and butter, that "no cake could taste
better !" The bread was made of good whole wheat flour,
stirred up with nothing but water, and baked in gem
irons. It was spread with creamery butter, and we think
any one to be pitied who would not like the taste of such
butter. Thorough chewing adds to the pleasure of the
sense of taste, this taste resides in the tongue, and in
the soft palate and its arches. One common way of
abusing the sense of taste is, by eating fast with very
slight chewing, so that the food is not retained in the

mouth long enough to give the nerves of taste a chance to fairly taste the quality of food eaten. But for this rapid eating, and washing down with agreeably flavored drinks, much that is usually eaten would be rejected as either bitter or tasteless.

AN "ANNEX" TO A COFFEE MILL.

Figure 114 shows a box to stand on an ordinary coffee mill to hold the coffee, and to measure the quantity required to be ground for each meal. The box is of three-eighths-inch stuff, has a cover at the top, and is of the proper size to fit the mill. Near the bottom of the box is the slide, of tin or sheet iron, shown in figure 115. When the box is filled with coffee, a single movement of the slide will let the required quantity down into the mill. The distance between the two arms of the slide is ascertained by placing the proper quantity of coffee in the box, marking the hight at which it stands, and

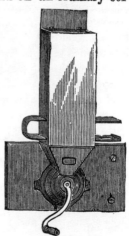

Fig. 114.—COFFEE MILL "ANNEX."

Fig. 115.—THE "SHUT OFF," OR SLIDE.

making the slot for the slide to work in at that place. The rest is clearly shown by the engraving.

SCOURING MITTEN.

These mittens, figure 116, which every house-keeper will think very useful little articles after she has tried them, are made of rubber cloth, cut the shape of a mitten, without the thumb, stitched two rows with the machine on the wrong side, and then turned. The mittens must be two sizes larger than an ordinary mitten. The rubber cloth can be bought at dry goods stores by the

Fig. 116.—SCOURING   Fig. 117.—SEALING WAX   Fig. 118.—CAKE
MITTEN.   CUP.   FUNNEL.

yard, and as it is impenetrable, it effectually protects the hands from the preparation used for scouring, and removes the most unpleasant feature of the work.

CUP FOR SEALING-WAX.

A large tin cup, with a broad, flat bottom, and spout, as shown in figure 117, is convenient for melting sealing-wax for fruit cans. The wax melts in it very quickly, and the spout is a great advantage.

FUNNEL FOR CAKE PAN.

When making certain kinds of cake, it is often desirable to use an earthen dish, so that all danger of a hard crust will be prevented. A tin funnel, figure 118, can be made to order at a tin shop, and with it any dish can be changed into a cake pan, as occasion demands.

WOOD-BOX.

Figure 119 shows a box for holding fire-wood, which has the advantage of being cheap and convenient. An ordinary dry-goods or other box is the basis, the cover being braced with cross slats and provided with hinges, so that it can be closed when desired. It is a common experience that the shovel, if not provided with a place, is often at the bottom of the wood in the box when wanted,

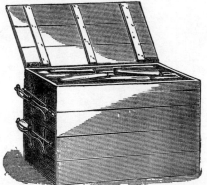

Fig. 119.—A CONVENIENT WOOD-BOX.

and the same may be said of the tongs. To remedy this trouble, four hooks—the same as used in closets for hanging up clothes—are fastened to the outside of the box, one pair for the shovel, and the other for the tongs to rest upon. A convenient place being thus provided for these tools, they should, and doubtless will, be found there. A coat of paint—lead-color is perhaps the best for the kitchen—will improve the appearance of the box.

A WOOD-BOX WITH DRAWER.

Wherever wood is burned, something to hold it is necessary, as a matter of neatness as well as to protect the floor and wall where the wood is placed. This box, shown in figure 120, should be of stuff not less than three-quarters of an inch thick, and all the better if of inch boards. The large compartment, for holding wood, is twenty-two inches high, fourteen inches wide, and twenty-two inches long, inside measurement. The side portion, *B*, with sloping lid, is ten inches deep, the same wide, and of course as long as the other portion. Below this is the drawer, *R*, shown partly open. For the kitchen the box may be

Fig. 120.—CONVENIENT WOOD-BOX.

painted, to conform to the general woodwork, but for other rooms a pleasing finish may be given by papering the exterior with wall-paper. Very clever imitations of oak, walnut, and other woods, are now made in wall-paper, some of which would be appropriate for such a use as this. Of course the large division is for wood, and it should be recollected that the durability of the box will depend much upon the care taken by the person who keeps it supplied. If the wood is dumped by the armful into the box with a crash, it will last but a short time. There is a right and a wrong way in so simple an operation as dropping an armful of wood. The drawer may be used for kindlings, and the compartment above as a receptacle for dust-pan and brush, stove-blacking, etc.; or these may go below and the kindlings above.

A CONVENIENT AND ORNAMENTAL WOOD-BOX.

The box stands on casters with a handle at each end and can be readily moved. The length is thirty-one inches,

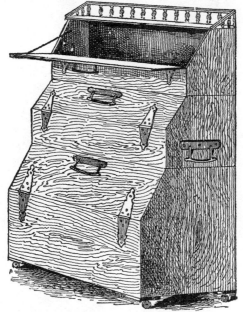

Fig. 121.—A CONVENIENT WOOD-BOX.

width seventeen inches, hight forty inches, without including the ornamental top. The lowest box is for large wood. The width is seventeen inches, hight nineteen inches, with a door ten inches wide. The middle box is for kindling. The width is ten inches, hight thirteen inches, with a door eight inches wide. The top box is for shavings or paper. The width is six inches, hight eight inches, with a door six inches wide. Short pieces of small chain are fastened to each door at one end, to hold it at a convenient angle when open; when they close, the chains drop into the box out of sight. The hinges and handles may be of ornamental brass or as plain as desired. The top is a convenient place for holding any useful article or ornament.

A NEAT WOOD-BOX.

The materials required in construction of the wood-box shown in figures 122, 123 and 124, are: about thirty feet

Fig. 122.—END VIEW.   Fig. 123.—FRONT VIEW OF WOOD-BOX.

one-inch white pine, six one and one-quarter inch No. 8 screws, one-half pound six-penny nails, a few brads, and one-half pound glue. Figure 122 shows an end view with center, from which the circle is drawn at *a*. Figure 123 is a front view, from which the ornamental back can easily be reproduced, figures 122 and 123 both being one-sixteenth of the actual size. Figure 124 is a perspective view not drawn to scale. Size of box, outside measure, twenty-six inches long, seventeen inches wide, fifteen inches high

Fig. 124—PERSPECTIVE VIEW OF WOOD-BOX.

in front, and twenty-three inches high behind to underside of the shelf, *b*. The shelf is twenty-eight inches long, and nine inches wide, molded on the ends and the front edge, projecting one inch. The ornamental back is cut from a piece twenty-seven and one-half inches long, and thirteen and one-half inches wide. At *c*, figure 124, is shown a drawer, four inches deep on the face, sliding under the shelf, *b*, on cleats fastened to the ends of the box, inside. At *d* is a movable till or box, which rests in place on shelf *b*, and is secured from slipping off by pins fastened in the shelf, which enter corresponding holes in the ends of the till. Handles to drawer and till are turned from black-walnut, and fastened securely by screws from the inside. The box is securely dove-tailed

together, front and back, as high as shelf *b*. The ornamental back-piece is then fastened by dowels and glue in
place. The shelf is then nailed on, nailing through the
back into the edge of the shelf. The bottom of the box
is then nailed on, and the drawer, constructed of the usual
pattern, is fitted to its place so as to slide in and out easily.
The till is constructed the same as the drawer, except the
front, which is made from one-quarter-inch clear, straight-
grained pine, steamed, and nailed with three-quarter-inch
brads, while hot, into its place. The movable till is very
convenient to use in gathering chips, or as a receptacle for
kindlings. It being as light and portable as a chip-basket,
and never in the way. The drawer is used to hold a stove-
brush, shovel, blacking, stove-hook, kindling-hatchet,
kindling-saw, hearth-broom, etc., being a place for the
stove utensils that are usually scattered under foot and out
of place. The drawer is not in the way of putting in or
taking out fuel, and the boys or men who keep the box
supplied, should be taught to place the wood in quietly
and regularly, and not to throw it into the box in a careless manner.

CANNING TOMATOES.

Many housewives think canning tomatoes is a mysterious and difficult operation. Here is a good method:
Place thoroughly ripe and sound tomatoes, a few at a time,
in a kettle of boiling water. As soon as the skins crack,
remove and peel the fruit, cutting out the hard stem part.
Place the tomatoes in a porcelain or granite-lined kettle
and boil steadily until the watery juice has evaporated.
Add for each gallon one heaping tablespoonful of salt,
and one-half teaspoonful of cayenne pepper. Dip a coarse
cloth in hot water, remove the rubber from the jar, dip it
in hot water, and replace it on the jar, lightly wring the

cloth, wrap it around the jar, set it in a pail or basin, with the surplus corners of the cloth under the jar, insert the canning-tunnel in the mouth of the jar, and with a common water dipper, fill the jar full of the boiling fruit. Place on the cover, screw it down tightly, and set the jar on a dry cloth, out of the draft to cool. When nearly cold, tighten the cover down once more. Keep the fruit in a cool, dark, dry cellar, in a board cupboard, resting on the ground.

RAT AND MOUSE TRAPS.

To make a good rat trap, take a barrel and support the head on pivots. A weight is fixed to one pivot to keep the head in position and a few grains of corn are glued on

Fig. 125.—MOUSE TRAP.

to the head. When a rat or mouse steps on the head, it turns and the animal drops into the barrel ; the weight immediately brings the head into position again. The trap (figure 125) is a smaller one for mice, made of wood

Fig. 126.—TRAP AT WORK.

or tin, on the same principle. These traps should for a few days be set in the haunts of the vermin, fixed so as not

to work, so that they will become accustomed to them.
Then set for use.   Figure 126 shows the trap in operation

AN UNPATENTED TRAP.

A bucket is fitted with a circular board or false cover,
which is so nicely suspended, that a slight weight upon
either side of the center will cause it to tilt.   The bait is

Fig. 127.—A MOUSE OR RAT-TRAP.

suspended by a wire in such a manner, that it can only
be reached from this treacherous platform.   The bucket
contains water for the reception of the rat or mouse.
Where rats are shy, as they will be where traps have been
frequently set, it is well to fix the platform so that it can-

not move, and allow them to take away the bait for a few times. When they have become accustomed to the affair, they may then be easily trapped. Figure 127 shows this bucket trap.

TOMATO CATSUP—TOMATO SAUCE.

The basis of Tomato Catsup, or Ketchup, is the pulp of ripe tomatoes. Many defer making catsup until late in the season, when the cool nights cause the fruit to ripen slowly, and it may be it is gathered hurriedly for fear of a frost. The late fruit does not yield so rich a pulp as that gathered in its prime. The fruit should have all green portions cut out, and be stewed gently until thoroughly cooked. The pulp is then to be separated from the skins, by rubbing through a wire sieve, so fine as to retain the seeds. The liquor thus obtained, is to be evaporated to a thick pulp, over a slow fire, and should be stirred to prevent scorching. The degree of evaporation will depend upon how thick it is desired to have the catsup. We prefer to make it so that it will just pour freely from the bottle. We observe no regular rule in flavoring. Use sufficient salt. Season with cloves, allspice, and mace, bruised and tied in a cloth, and boiled in the pulp; add a small quantity of powdered cayenne. Some add the spices, ground fine, directly to the pulp. A clove of garlic, bruised and tied in a cloth, to be boiled with the spices, imparts a delicious flavor. Some evaporate the pulp to a greater thickness than is needed, and then thin with vinegar or with wine. An excellent and useful tomato sauce may be made by preparing the pulp, but adding no spices, and putting it in small bottles while hot, corking securely and sealing. If desired, the sauce may be salted before bottling, but this is not essential. To add to soups, stews, sauces and

6

made dishes, a sauce thus prepared is an excellent substitute for the fresh fruit. It should be put in small bottles, containing as much as will be wanted at once, as it will not keep long after opening.

EASILY MADE STEPS.

Figure 128 shows a step-stand, which has two important qualities, viz.: a broad place to stand upon at top, and it can be easily and cheaply made. It is a step-stand which has no means for folding up and lengthening out, is substantial and safe, and is not patented. The engraving

shows how it is made. It may be of any size, but one that will pass readily through an ordinary door, and is about three feet in hight, will be very convenient. If the legs are made of hardwood, they need not be very large, and the braces, which serve as steps on the front side, can be nailed, but it is better to

Fig. 128.—A STEP-STAND.　　screw them, to the legs. The top should be so large that a person can stand upon it, with room for a pail. The three short braces beneath the top are not shown in the engraving, but should not be omitted in the construction. This step-stand may be made by any one who can use a saw and drive a nail. Many families who can not afford to buy a step-ladder from the stores, can build one for the few cents the lumber and nails, or screws, will cost. Aside from the household, such a step-stand will serve a good purpose in picking fruit.

WOODEN FRUIT KNIVES, ETC.

Men folks who pare fruits, and whose incisors, if they have them, do not easily break into the side of a large hard apple, resort to the pocket knife. But it goes against the grain to cut fruit with a blade which has just cleaned a hoof, skinned an animal, and often been used for other unclean operations. Here is a remedy. Any bit of hard-wood whittled to a sharp edge, in half a minute, will pare and cut an apple, however hard, almost as

Fig. 129.—WOODEN FRUIT KNIFE.

well as a steel blade. It can be thrown away, or easily washed, or cleaned by taking off an extra shaving, and when dulled be sharpened in the same way. The sketch (figure 129) shows an extempore knife made of a stick from the kindling wood box, with three strokes of a pocket jack-knife, and in ten seconds. It has pared, cut and cored a number of quite hard apples very effectually.

CANNING FRUITS AND VEGETABLES.

American house-keepers are not aware of the great advantages they enjoy over their European cousins in the matter of canning. It is not many years since the representative of one of the leading London journals, who was on a visit to this country, found this one of the most interesting things that he noticed on his trip. Wherever he went he found the ladies of the household engaged in canning fruit—a thing then unknown in England. The American house-keeper accepts canning as a part of the regular household routine, and it in a great measure takes the place of the old "preserving" time. To suc-

cessfully put up fruits and vegetables, the great essential
is glass jars, or cans, that are readily made air-tight.
These are now supplied by manufacturers, several patterns of them, in a form so complete that there is little
practical difference among them. The jars of the leading
makers of the present day are well-nigh perfect, and we
do not know of any choice between them. Having the
cans, or jars, the operation is simple. The fruit, whatever it may be, in a syrup just strong enough to properly
sweeten it, is brought to the boiling point, and when the
air has all been expelled from it, it is at once placed in the
jars, previously warmed with hot water, and when these
are well-filled, the cover is screwed down tight. Good
jars, well filled with boiling fruit, and promptly covered
by screwing down the caps, will insure success. Among
the first things to be canned in this manner, is Rhubarb.
This can be readily canned, and green Gooseberries may
be treated in the same manner. Strawberries and Rasp-
berries come next, and are better preserved in the same
manner than by any other, but these, especially the Strawberry, while vastly better when preserved thus than in
any other manner, come far short of retaining their
original flavor. Peaches are easily preserved thus, and
are nearly perfect, as are pears, especially the Bartlett,
apples and quinces. One who has canned the quince in
this manner, will never preserve it according to the old
pound for pound method. All the highly flavored apples,
preserved by canning, make a finer apple sauce than can
be produced in any other manner. The usual process is,
to cook the fruit, of whatever kind, in a syrup made
with four ounces of sugar to a pint of water. When the
fruit is cooked tender, transfer it at once to the jar, and
add the syrup to fill up every crevice ; if there are bubbles
of air, aid them to escape, by the use of a spoon ; see that
the jar is solid full of fruit and syrup, and up to the top,
before the cap is screwed on. While fruits are easily pre-

served in the family, vegetables are more difficult. There
are many inquiries about preserving green peas, green
corn, and tomatoes. Those who make a business of canning, find green peas and green corn among the most difficult things to preserve. They can only be put up in tin
cans by long boiling processes, not practicable in families.
If any housewife has found a method by which either
corn or peas can be preserved by any process practicable
in the family, she should communicate it for the
benefit of others. We recently made an experiment
with tomatoes. Thoroughly ripe fruit was cooked as for
the table, omitting butter and all other seasoning, and
placed in ordinary fruit jars. About three out of twelve
failed, but those which succeeded were vastly better than
the tomatoes purchased in tin cans.

CORN-COB CRATE.

From two-thirds to seven-eighths of all the cobs obtained
from home-shelled corn in Minnesota, Dakota, Nebraska,
Kansas, and in North Missouri and Central Iowa, are
saved for and used as fuel. There are thousands of families who employ no other fuel, except in very cold
weather, though the well-to-do burn both coal and corn-
cobs. Usually, the cobs are housed, to keep them dry,
but in too many instances they are left out in the rain,
and absorb so much moisture as to destroy half their
value for fuel. The crate, holding a day's supply of cobs
for a large stove, is made of half-inch siding, tin or
sheet-iron ; the latter preferably to avoid dust. It is
three feet high and two feet square. There is an opening
near the bottom through which the cobs are taken out.
The crate is placed on a stand, having vertical legs of any
desired length, or as long as is necessary to bring the top
of the stand on a level with the top of the stove. On the

sides of this stand or table the side strips are raised half
an inch above the level of the top surface to keep the
crate from sliding off.   A bottom board to the stand may
hold pail, basket, or dishes.   There may be a drawer for
knives or other kitchen utensils.   The crate can be taken
off at any time when not in use, and the stand used as
a sewing table.

HEATING WATER—A JAPAN BATH.

A Japan Bath is shown in figure 130.   Such an affair
would be much used in this country if it were generally

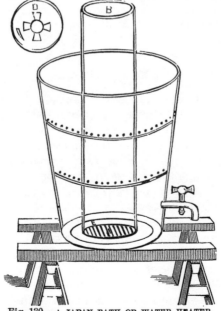

Fig. 130.—A JAPAN BATH OR WATER HEATER.

known how quickly and cheaply water can be heated in
it.   The reservoir used is a half-barrel, large firkin, or

some such affair. In the center is a cylinder of sheet iron, *B*, which fits over a hole in the bottom of the vessel; it has a flange, *E*, at the bottom, by means of which it is fastened to the bottom of the barrel, by rivets, with red-lead between the two to make a close joint; there is a grate, *A*, at the bottom of the cylinder, to hold the charcoal. At the top is a cover, *D*, with openings that may be closed more or less, and serve as a damper. A faucet near the bottom completes the heater. It should be set upon two horses or other supports, placed far enough apart to clear the grate and allow the coals that may drop from it to fall to the ground. Our correspondent states that, properly managed, two pounds of charcoal is enough fuel for a day.

STRAWBERRY SHORT-CAKE.

If one partakes of Strawberry Short-Cake in half a dozen different cafes, it is likely that a different preparation will be served at each. The old-fashioned Shortcake is in many places replaced by a kind of confectionery, made with slices of cake (somewhat like pound-cake) covered with whipped cream, in which a few strawberries are imbedded. This is quite unlike the real thing. Among the recipes for Short-Cake that have been tried, the following was preferred: flour, one quart; butter three tablespoonfuls; buttermilk (or rich sour milk), one large cupful; one egg; white sugar (powdered), one tablespoonful; soda (dissolved in warm water), one teaspoonful; salt one saltspoonful. Mix the salt and sugar with the flour; chop up the butter in the flour; add the egg and soda to the milk and mix, handling as little as possible. Roll out lightly, lay one sheet of paste upon the other in a round tin and bake. While still warm, separate the cakes, and place between them a thick layer of strawberries, which should

be abundantly sugared.   Some place a layer of the fruit
on the upper cake.   It is eaten with sugar and cream.

EGG TESTER.

A bad egg is never welcome, and any simple device
that will quickly and satisfactorily detect the quality of
an egg, is important.   A very simple method used by

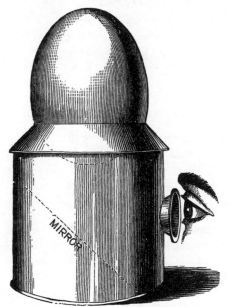

Fig. 131.—A "CUP" EGG TESTER.

many is to so hold the egg that the hand cuts off all
direct rays of light from the eye, except those passing
through the egg.   The egg may be held towards the sun,
or better, towards the light from a lighted candle or lamp
in a dark room.   Figure 131 shows a tester.   It is a small

tin cup three inches high, and two and a half inches in diameter, narrowed in at the top to hold an egg endwise. A small mirror is placed as shown by the dotted line. The light passes through the egg, and forms an image upon the mirror which is distinctly seen at the side opening. The same principle is used in the tester shown in figure 132, and more than one egg is examined at once. This is a small, low box, either of wood or paste board,

Fig. 132.—A BOX EGG TESTER.

with a number of "egg holes" cut in the cover. A mirror is placed within, and one side of the box is cut away for observation. If the interior of the box is painted black, the effect will be better. The quality of egg is determined by their degree of clearness. A good egg shows a clear reddish translucent light. The ease with which testers can be made and used, should insure good eggs for the table, and fertile ones for incubation.

CHAPTER IV.

PANTRIES, CLOSETS AND CUPBOARDS.

A CUPBOARD UNDER A CHIMNEY.

A cupboard is shown in figure 133 which can be built

Fig. 133.—CUPBOARD FOR DRAWERS UNDER CHIMNEY.

under a chimney if the latter does not extend into
the cellar. Such a cupboard takes up no available

room.   It might be made with shelves, all the way down, instead of with drawers and shelves, but the latter are convenient, and well worth the little extra expense.   The cupboard may be made of pine boards, nicely joined, and oiled to match the rest of the woodwork in the kitchen.

CORNER CUPBOARD AND DRYING LINE.

Two very convenient things in a kitchen are, a cupboard in the chimney corner, and a wire line around the

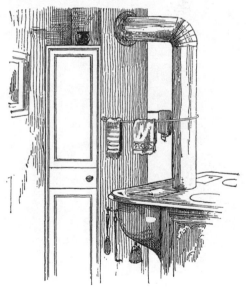

Fig. 134—CUPBOARD AND LINE.

stove pipe, on which the dish towels are dried (figure 134).   The line, which is of copper wire, is fastened by screwing hooks in each side of the chimney, and stretching the wire from one side to another.   The line will bear considerable weight without sagging.

The cupboard is built in the corner made by the chimney, which extends down into the wash-room in the cellar below, and is fitted up with shelves for holding such things as are in constant use about the stove when cooking is in progress. Unless there is a door in the way, another cupboard on the other side of the chimney will make a good place for storing away seeds, and things generally which should be kept dry.

A WELL-ARRANGED PANTRY.

In figure 135 is shown a portion of a pantry that is well arranged and convenient. The window is placed at the end of the room, while around three sides is built a shelf,

Fig. 135.—A COMMODIOUS AND WELL ARRANGED PANTRY.

thirty inches in hight, and from fifteen to twenty inches wide. Beneath this shelf are placed drawers, cupboards, shelves, etc. The shelf situated in the end of the pantry is left unobstructed for cutting meat, bread, mixing pastry, and even for washing dishes. It will be found the most convenient and most used part of the whole room, being near the light, and with plenty of space. At either side of the pantry are arranged other cupboards, shelves, drawers, etc., in any manner thought most convenient, and are used for holding table linen, glassware, china, silver, etc., while those near the floor are for kettles, pans, pails, and other coarse kitchen ware. Some may think ten or a dozen drawers are far too many for one pantry, but in practice, more, instead of a less number, could be economically used. It is best to furnish some of the drawers with locks and keys, that they may be securely fastened when desired. Paint the wood-work in some light color ; it is better to simply oil the top of the shelf near the window with raw linseed oil, as the paint soon wears off.

A POISON BOX.

The use of poisons for the destruction of insects, and other purposes, is so frequent, that all possible precau-

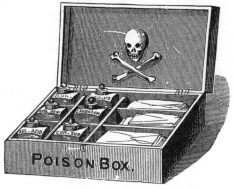

Fig. 136.—A BOX FOR EVERY HOUSEHOLD.

tions should be taken that these deadly agents do not destroy the life of members of the family. All poisons should be placed by themselves in a poison box (figure 136) and the box set where no one can get at it unless specially sought for. The many mistakes in administering a poison instead of a remedy, should teach that poisons should never be placed near the harmless medicines. Glaring labels are not enough, the poisons should have an out-of-the-way place of their own, and always kept there.

BOXES FOR THE STORE-ROOM.

It often happens that one wishes to use a place as a temporary store-room, and does not care to go to the

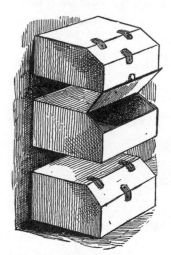

Fig. 137.—STORE-ROOM BOXES.

trouble or expense of fitting it up with substantial shelves or drawers. In such a case boxes arranged as shown in figure 137 will be found very useful. They occupy but little more space, and are almost as convenient as drawers. The front of the boxes are cut off and lids fastened on with leather hinges. A little strap of leather, tacked to the front of the lid, has a hole cut in the other end so it can be slipped over a knob on the front of the box to hold the lid securely shut, or over one in the box above to hold the lid up while putting things in and out of the box. The boxes are fastened securely to the wall by screws. Such boxes placed up in the attic are excellent for storing away seeds, herbs, clothes, carpet-rags, and anything which needs to be protected from dust or mice.

CHAPTER V.

THE DINING ROOM.

A CASE FOR SILVER SPOONS AND FORKS.

For the house-keeper who is fortunate enough to possess more forks, spoons, or knives, than she has in daily use, the little case shown in figure 138, is convenient. It is made of white drilling. Cut one piece double thickness, three inches wider than the length of the article (knife,

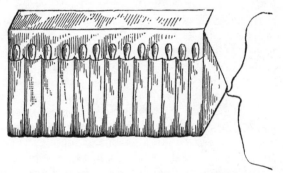

Fig. 138.—A CASE FOR SILVER TABLE WARE.

fork, or spoon), it is intended to hold, and long enough for twelve pockets and for a pointed flap at one end. Also one piece the length of the first, without the pointed flap, and not as wide by four inches. Run the larger piece together and turn it. Hem the smaller piece across the top, and baste it to the larger one. Stitch twelve casings large enough to let the article slip in easily, and bind all around with linen braid. Use the extra width of the back for a flap to turn over the top of the pocket. Sew strings to the pointed flap to tie the case.

Silver kept in a case does not tarnish so quickly as when it is scattered around in a drawer or on a shelf.

SHARPEN THE SHEARS, SCISSORS, KNIVES, ETC.

How the "men folks" would fret and sweat, grumble and growl, if they had to chop, mow, or whittle, or do any cutting, with blunt or round edge implements. Yet nine out of ten of "women folks" do most of their cutting up of meats with dull knives—round edged, made barely usable by rubbing them on a stove top—with an outlay of unnecessary strength and patience ; bread slices are haggled into thick and thin forms, with dull, over-thick knives ; long beating instead of cutting the hash meat fine.   It makes one ache—as badly as their hands or fingers ache—to see women trying to go through or shape a piece of cloth with shears or scissors, loose or rickety at the joints, and as for cutting edges on the blades, there are none.....The remedy is, first, we would say, let every woman, young or old, learn to sharpen implements, if necessary taking lessons of the men folks, or some one else. Second, let every man, who is a man, having a house and deserving one, give personal attention to the household cutting implements.   Ten minutes a week, or twenty minutes a month, of an evening or rainy day, will suffice to sharpen the shears and scissors clear to their points, tighten the joints to make the blades meet through their whole length—not so tightly as to strain the fingers, or so loosely as to let the cloth through uncut.   Also, to grind off the round of the kitchen cutting and chopping knives, and put an edge on them ; ditto the table knives.   Sharp table knives greatly help and save the teeth, save time in eating, while very finely cut meats, afterwards masticated long enough to mix them well

with saliva, digest far more easily, digest more thoroughly, and nourish and strengthen one much more. Sharpening knives often, pays well. They soon dull in cutting upon porcelain or China plates. In the absence of
a good sharpening steel, a case knife can be fairly sharpened on the bottom edge of a dinner plate. A thought-
full "head of the house" of our acquaintance often steps
into the dining room in advance of the bell call, and
quietly sharpens all the knives—especially if he has a sus-
picion that the steak or roast is not of the tenderest cut
or cooking, and especially if company is to be present.

A SIDE TABLE.

It is often that the one who presides at the table must
also be her own waiter there, and it is very annoying to
her, and to the guests, to be obliged to leave her seat

Fig. 139.—A COMMON SIDE TABLE.

every now and then to get some needed article, or to
change the plates. Much of this unpleasant movement
may be avoided by the use of a low side table; we have

heard this called a "dumb waiter," a name which belongs to a different affair; the French call it a *servante*. Figure 139 shows a convenient form for an arrangement of this kind; the size may be larger or smaller, according to that of the table itself. It should be strong and solid, and provided with casters, to allow it to be easily moved. The shelves below are important; they increase the holding capacity, and allow soiled dishes, etc., to be set out of sight. We have seen an excellent makeshift made from a box of convenient size, placed upon rollers; in this there was a shelf, which, with the bottom and top of the box, afforded three places to hold articles. A strip around three sides of the top will be useful to keep articles from slipping off. A common box, with the sides neatly upholstered with some material of quiet color, and the top, shelf, etc., covered with oilcloth, would answer. These side tables are very common in city homes.

THERMOMETERS.

The weather is said to be the only question upon which we can all agree ; but a little observation will show that this is no exception to the general rule of being subject to differences of opinion. Heat and cold are but relative terms, to be decided by each individual. Where one person is cold, his next neighbor, under the same circumstances, may be warm, and there is but one way of deciding just how warm or cold it really is, and that is to leave it to a third party which is without feelings, and upon whose decision we can all agree. Such is a thermometer. How often in the times of extremes of temperature we may hear the expression: "I only wish I knew how hot it has been to-day !" or, "I wonder how cold it was last night!" Aside from the simple pleasure to be derived from having a thermometer, it is of great use in giving us a true knowledge of the heat of our rooms, at any moment, thus aiding us in keeping them of the proper temperature—of about sixty-eight degrees. It is a good plan for young people to be taught to do something at a particular time, and to make and set down daily observations of the temperature will encourage regular habits, while the record will possess sufficient interest to compensate for the trouble. Thermometers are now so cheap, that everybody may possess one ; those of low price are quite as likely to be accurate as those with an ornamental mounting. The excellence of the instrument depends upon having the tube of equal bore throughout, and the care with which the degrees are marked upon the scale.

TABLE DECORATION.

In any decoration, whether for a private or a public table, heaviness should be avoided, and lightness and grace characterize every design, whether large or small. The matter of home decoration is easily managed, and may be dismissed by saying—the simpler the better. It often happens that parties, festivals, and other social gatherings take place during the season of flowers, at which refreshments are served. Those having charge of the table arrangements naturally desire to decorate with flowers, and usually make the mistake of having these in great quantity, without bestowing any care upon the arrangement. A crowded bouquet in any place is less pleasing than a loose and graceful one, and this is especially the case in table decorations. Where persons are to be seated at the table, it is especially important that the decorations should not be so heavy as to obstruct the view from one side to the other. Light, feathery foliage and delicate vines should form the chief material of all table decoration, and flowers may come in for color, but

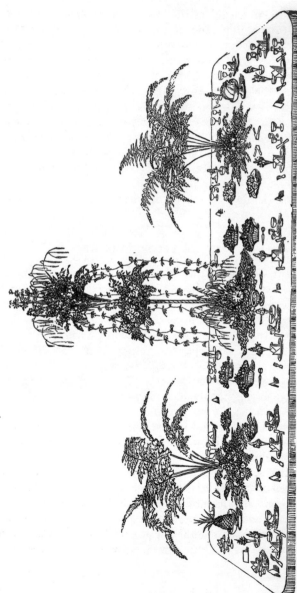

Fig. 140.—PRIZE DESIGN FOR TABLE DECORATION AT THE ROYAL HORTICULTURAL SOCIETY, ENGLAND.

not, as is too often the case, to make up the mass. One with a little ingenuity and skill can make up tasteful decorations from very ordinary materials. If elevated stands are wanted, and glass ones can not be procured, let the tinman make the portions to hold the flowers (to be filled with wet moss), and support them on glass rods. Even wooden supports may be used, if quite clothed with vines. In the country an abundance of ferns may be had for the searching, and they can be largely used in such work. The leaves of carrots, parsley, and the common yarrow are not to be rejected. The young growth of grape and hop vines, with the spray of asparagus, will, under a skillful hand, work into pleasing forms, and the common green-brier may be turned to good account. The green groundwork being secured, then flowers may be sparingly worked in. If no flowering vines are at hand, those that do not bear flowers may be made to do so by binding to them carnations and other flowers that hold well without water, by means of a very fine iron wire. By the exercise of a little ingenuity a table for a summer festival, shown in figure 140, can be made beautiful by the use of common materials.

INEXPENSIVE DECORATIONS.

It is quite wonderful how common things and materials are being utilized for home-decoration, and art work of all kinds. This only shows the fertility of the human brain, in designing something new and strange ; and the hold which the so-called " æsthetic craze" has taken upon the community. Unbleached muslin, cheese-cloth, and cotton flannel have each had their day, and now woollen blankets are taking their turn. These, when dyed in rich colors, and embroidered in silk and crewel, certainly make most luxurious sofa-coverings, handsome enough for any drawing-room that can be found.

A warm looking portiere, is made of a claret-red blanket, banded with plush of a deeper shade, and decorated with old-gold crewel work.   Another blanket, dyed blue, bound with a darker blue velveteen, and handsomely outlined in sunflowers or other designs, forms a most elegant rug for the carriage.

In some of the finest houses in England, the walls of dining-rooms are now covered with common brown wrapping paper, such as is used for doing up parcels ; and the effect is said to be very good, when combined with a highly decorative frieze.   A good idea is to cover an old wooden mantel-piece, or screen, with this coarse paper, and paint in oil, with large and effective designs of red poppies, or cat-tails.   One of the most popular styles now of amateur work, is pen-and-ink etching on linen.   Until recently, black indelible ink was the only kind that could be procured ; but it now comes in several brilliant and permanent colors—scarlet,   blue,   brown,   violet,   green,   and crimson.   These inks are accompanied by a mordant, or preparation for setting the dye, with which the cloth should first be saturated, then dried, and ironed smooth. Any dainty figure, initial, or monogram may be used, and this style of ornamentation is peculiarly suitable for napkins, towels, and doilys, and we have seen pillow shams decorated in the same manner.

If you have a correct eye, and can draw well, so much the better ; but if not, select any small picture with few lines, such as can be found in many children's books ; or a Japanese bird or figure.   Place a thin paper over it, trace the outline and prick the lines of your tracing carefully with a fine needle.   Baste this pattern, rough side uppermost, on the linen, and rub a little charcoal powder over it, with a wad of soft cotton-wool.   Lift off the paper, and follow the dotted lines with a sharp pencil.

Blow off the powder, and you will then have a stamped design to work on with pen and ink. Draw very lightly and delicately, and if a solid effect is desired, it may be gained by light crossings, or parallel lines. When the decoration is completed, allow it to dry for an hour, and then lay the article flat for a few moments in a bowl of hot water, to take out the mordant and superfluous ink; after which it must be rinsed, dried and ironed.

This will be found very pretty and fascinating work, and is exceedingly durable, which is more than can be said of the outline work done in washing-silks, in which we have been much disappointed. A new fashion for marking handkerchiefs, is to write your autograph across the corner in pencil, and then work it over neatly in hem-stitch.

EXTENSION LEAF FOR A COMMON TABLE.

It is often desirable to extend or enlarge a common side-leaf table, and this may be readily done by a con-

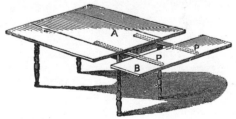

Fig. 141.—EXTRA LEAF FOR TABLE.

trivance shown in figure 141. This shows a board, B, about eighteen inches wide, and as long as the table is wide. Two hard-wood sticks, P, P, one inch square and three feet long, are secured to the leaf B by screws; two holes one inch square are made in the end close under top A, through which the supports P, P, pass as indi-

cated by dotted lines.   This is a very convenient method
of attaching a portable leaf, the only objection being the
disfigurement of the table by the two square holes.   To
avoid this, we would suggest the plan shown in figure 142,
in which *W, W,* are the side-leaves, and *E* the extra or

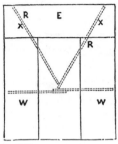

Fig. 142.—TABLE EXTENDED.

portable leaf, which is connected with the table by swinging arms *R, R,* loosely attached to leaf *E,* each by one
small bolt, placed near *X, X,* in the figure.   When in use,
the arms, *R, R,* are in the position indicated by dotted
lines, when not in use, fold lengthwise of the leaf and
occupy but little room.

"JUST FOR LOOKS."

A little boy was playing around the table set for dinner,
busily arranging several spoons which he had taken from
the side-board.   "What is that for?" inquired his
mother.   "Oh," said the little fellow, in an apologetic
tone, "just for looks."   There was an idea in the child's
mind, an element which, if properly directed, would grow
into something well calculated to give pleasure to himself
and others.   There often appears in individuals, and
even in some whole communities, particularly rural ones,
a seeming contempt for any improvement that is made

"just for looks." City regulations provide for the removal of garbage, and compel householders to be careful as to unsightly objects on the premises; but in villages and agricultural districts these matters are not so closely looked after by boards and corporations. The householder who "just for looks" is careful about emptying slops in the back yard, and the various odds and ends which accumulate about the premises, is not only instituting neatness and order, pleasant to the eye, but doing a good work for the health of her own home and neighborhood. Within doors, we would advocate many little things, for whose doing we can give no other reason than, "just for looks." A very little management makes the table pleasant to the eye; not merely a place at which we gather to eat. Expensive adornments are not essential. It requires no more time to set dishes straight than crooked. Not only does attention to outside appearances beautify the home, but it pays as well. The painted fence about an enclosure will last longer than an unpainted one. The gate swinging free upon its hinges is certainly more lasting than if suffered to drag upon the ground, uttering a most inhospitable welcome to the visitor. The scraper at the step and mat at the door, for muddy feet, the tasteful wall-basket for loose papers, the neatly-covered shoe-box, serving for a seat as well—are all little things of great value. If there are children in the household, this attention to appearances will exert more influence than many are aware of. The little one required to have clean hands and smooth hair before sitting down to a meal, is not very apt to grow up a man or woman careless of personal neatness. This attention to small things is not an evidence of mental smallness. A sense of order, a conviction of the morality of cleanliness, a nice development of taste, may not be given in the same degree to each one, but in beautifying our homes, in giving due regard to the adornment of our persons, in seeking out various con-

7

veniences, which often prove amenities of life, if we can act upon no better principle, let us do it "just for looks."

HOW TO CARVE A TURKEY.

It is easy for almost any one to learn how to divide a turkey respectably, but to do it skillfully is an accomplishment which can only be acquired by those who have a talent in that direction. Every boy—indeed, every girl, should learn to carve. In carving a turkey, as there is considerable difference in practice as to details—we will briefly give a method in carving for a family not large enough to require the whole turkey at one meal. For a

Fig. 143.—CARVING A TURKEY.

large company, a skillful carver places his fork in the bird, and does not remove it until the whole is divided; and in carving but one side, all cutting should be done before taking out the fork. The turkey, having all strings and skewers used in trussing removed, is placed on the table with its head (or neck) at the carver's left hand. A skilled carver will not rise from his seat, but most persons find it more convenient to stand while carving. First insert the fork firmly, as indicated in figure 143; then remove the whole leg and thigh by a cut shown at *a;* next remove the wing by a cut, as at *b*, letting these parts lie on the platter. Then cut downwards as many slices from the breast—the white meat—as there are persons to be served (as shown by the lines at *c*); then make an opening into the cavity of the bird at a place now hidden by the leg, for dipping out the stuffing. Next separate the leg (drumstick) from the thigh, or second joint; the platter should be large enough to allow this to be done upon it, but if there is not room, a plate must be used. To hit the joint, notice the movements in an uncooked turkey; it is indicated by a line in figure 144, and the separation is easily made with the right cut. The thigh, or second joint, should yield at least three portions; one with the bone, and two without, and a piece of this, with a slice from the breast served, unless some one is known to prefer a part of the drumstick — as many do — the thigh

Fig. 144.—A LEG.

and drumstick will usually make three portions of dark meat, each ; some prefer all white meat, and their liking, if not known, should be asked. Always lay the pieces outer, or skin side up, and add a small spoonful of stuffing. Unless the preferences are known, it is proper to ask if stuffing will be taken. The carver's task ends with supplying each one as above mentioned, and the plate goes to the server of vegetables. If there is an old person present, or one known to be particular as to food on account of imperfect teeth, there is a choice bit just below where the thigh is removed, known to many as the " tenderloin," which is easily removed. The side-bone, which many carvers reserve for themselves, is removed by placing the knife in close to the rump and pressing it towards the head, when a thin plate of bone will come away with some choice pickings upon it. The wish-bone may be removed by cutting down from above, as shown at *d, d*. There is a side bone to which the wing is attached, the removal of which is not difficult, but it cannot well be described. The wing gives one good cut, that nearest the body, and this may be served as white meat. If one side of the turkey is not enough for the company, the other is to be proceeded with in the same manner. The best way to learn to carve is to carefully watch an expert, and note his operations. A close examination of the turkey before it is cooked will help in giving a knowledge of the position of the joints.

TOO MUCH SUGAR!

Sugar is a useful article of diet, yet the ancients lived very comfortably without it. The people of England were without sugar until the fourteenth century. Though sugar is found in nearly all of the fruits, vegetables, seeds, and meats that constitute our food, it would be very inconvenient to be deprived of the manufactured and refined sugar. There is perhaps nothing we eat that works more mischief, especially with the liver and kidneys, than sugar used in excess. The evil begins in babyhood, when the milk or gruel for baby's bottle is unduly sweetened. Too starchy food may also produce unpleasant results, as it is one cause and aggravation of some diseases of the kidneys. After considerable experience with healthy children who seldom showed any great thirst for water in infancy, and who were not fed sugar or candy or sweetened food when very young, we are to believe that when little ones keep calling frequently for water, it is because they have been improperly fed, and the irritated stomach demands the cooling influence of water to allay its tendency to inflammation.

A mother often complains that her child is troubled greatly with a sour stomach, but this case is no longer mysterious when the mother, to quiet the little one, so that she can continue her account of the case, sets down before her a little dish of sugar, from which the child may help itself. Most mothers would give candy or a cookie instead, though some feed their children lumps of sugar from the bowl, believing that the children need sugar, and might better have it in that form than any other. In any case of this kind there is a very frequent call for water.

Do you know how vinegar is made ? You can get plenty of it by simply mixing sugar or molasses with water and keeping it warm. A sour taste in the mouth after eating sweets, is of very common occurrence. It is the acid caused by the fermentation of the sugar left in the mouth, with the saliva that causes the decay of children's teeth—this and the lack of bone-forming material in the daily food. Vinegar " eats " lime, as one can tell by leaving an egg in vinegar. Bits of sugar or candy left to ferment among the teeth, destroy their enamel as well as do pickles. The child that is fed on sweets, naturally craves pickles as an antidote, but well-fed children are contented with plain nourishing food, if properly prepared and sufficiently varied. Many imagine that all children should have free access to both sugar and pickles, in order to supply what they suppose to be natural cravings, and to prevent thefts of sugar from the family bowl. This is a mistaken policy.

MAKING THE TABLE ATTRACTIVE.

In matters of the table, the question how far the eye shall be gratified as well as the palate, must be decided by the circumstances of each house-keeper. We cannot expect the farmer's wife who, with several children to care for, has to provide the three meals a day for her husband and several hired men, to look much after the ornamentation of the table. If she can provide a fairly clean table-cloth, and tolerably bright knives, forks, and spoons, she does well. Indeed, these are the very foundation of

all table adornment, for where these are wanting all
ornamentation of dishes is out of place.   There is a
great deal in the way of doing little things, and one

Fig. 145.—A LEAF OF THE FERN-LEAVED PARSLEY.

house-keeper will have her table neat and attractive,
while that of another, with exactly the same means, will
be the reverse.   For example, a handful of radishes,

thrown higledy-pigledy upon a plate, all heads and points, looks careless. The very same radishes, placed in a tumbler or other glass, with the neatly cut tops all uppermost, make a pleasing ornament for the table. If cold meat is to be served for supper or tea, it makes a wonderful difference whether the remains of the leg of mutton is set on as they were left at dinner, and perhaps in the same dish, or a few thin slices cut off, and neatly laid upon a plate. But these things, it may be said, come under the head of order and neatness, and have nothing to do with garnishing. With many housekeepers order and neatness are all that they can hope to secure, and fortunate is the hard-worked farmer's wife, if she can always welcome her husband after his day's work, to a table adorned by these. There are, however, many among our readers who can go a step in the direction of ornamentation of the table. If there are strawberries for tea—as there should be in every farm house in the season, the farmer's wife may well spend a few minutes in placing strawberry leaves around the edge of the dish, no matter how common the ware. If there are grapes for dessert, a few leaves and tendrils among the clusters give an easily added beauty. A house-keeper who cares to make her table attractive will find it a great help to have a few roots of parsley in the garden in summer, or in a box of earth in the kitchen window in winter. It is a small matter, to be sure, but the brightness that a few green leaves, contrasted with the white china and white table-cloth, bring to the table, is worth just the little trouble required to secure it. A few leaves of parsley around any dish of cold meats converts it into an object of beauty. We mention parsley, because it is the green the most generally used and the most easily provided. The seeds take a long while to come up, but the plants, when established, grow freely in any garden soil. Of late, a variety has been introduced called

"Fern-leaved," of which a single leaf is shown in the engraving. This is as easily grown as the common parsley, but it is so beautifully cut and frilled and fringed, that it is handsome enough to serve as the green to the finest bouquet. A box of it in the kitchen forms a cheerful ornament, and its leaves will be at hand when wanted. Of course parsley is not the only material that may be used for garnishing dishes. A few slices of beet and carrot, cut crosswise, will set off a dish of sliced corned beef; sliced, hard-boiled eggs may be used to ornament a salad, etc.

CHAPTER VI.

THE SITTING ROOM.

FANCY ARTICLES.

Art in every form, and particularly in house decoration, is seemingly carrying everything before it, and every month brings out richer, and more magnificent designs in painting and embroidery. Plush and velvet are favorite materials, for the groundwork, and make the richest backgrounds for the exquisite sprays of flowers, flying birds, or æsthetic figures thrown upon them.

One handsome chair that we have seen, was of wicker-ware, and had luxurious cushions for the seat and back, of crimson silk plush, upon which snow-balls were embroidered in the new-raised work, now so fashionable. This is done by cutting short bits of silk or crewels and sewing them in, a few at a time. It is a long and rather tedious task, but superb when completed. The popular design of golden rod is done in the same manner.

An oriental-looking scrap-bag is made of four Japanese pictures, joined together by red, yellow and blue bands, crocheted of single zephyr or shetland wool. A bag of any material desired—Cretonne or Silesia is pretty—is fitted in the bottom, and a gay border is placed around the top, which is drawn up with a cord, and the whole is finished off with dainty little tassels at each corner. They somewhat resemble Chinese lanterns, and are very useful. A convenient trifle for a house-keeper is a ball of twine fitted in a knitted case of bright-colored work—like the soft parlor balls used by young children—but with a hole at the bottom, through which the string passes and un-winds from it the inside of the ball.   Suspended from it is a small pair of scissors on a narrow satin ribbon—loops of the same ribbon being used to hang it on the wall, where it will always be at hand, when there is a parcel to be tied up.   Dried grasses, leaves, and berries are much used in decorating fancy baskets, shaving-paper cases, etc;, and gilded acorns are frequently seen.   At a recent church sale, sprays of natural flowers arranged on large palm-leaf fans sold readily, while tasteful winter bou-quets were shown of bitter-sweet on a background of evergreens, tied with bows of light ribbon.   The lam-brequins of Macremé lace still hold their own, but the ty-ing of the knots is so hard on the hands, that many pre-fer to crochet them of fish-twine, which is very quickly done and exceedingly pretty when lined with some bright color or ribbon run through the openings.   Ladies bags and shopping-bags are also crocheted of the fish-twine, which comes much cheaper than the flax used for the real Macremé lace.

A PLEASING LAMP SHADE.

The shade figure 146 is made of six pieces of perforated cardboard, of the shape shown in the engraving.   The pieces are six inches long, five and a half inches wide

below, and three inches above.   Each of these bound all
around with narrow dark-green ribbon and the pieces
attached to one another by a few stitches above and below
through the ribbon.   The whole may be folded, and
occupy but small space when not in use.   Each piece is

Fig. 146.—DECORATED LAMP SHADE.

ornamented by autumn leaves, bits of fern and moss;
these are sewed to hold them firmly.   Either oil the
leaves, or dip them in paraffine.   A screen of this kind,
before the leaves fade, presents a rich variety of colors.

OLD FURNITURE.

As a nation, we are not lovers of old things, but we
run after those that are novel.   We set to one side anything that is at all old, and say it has had its day.   This
spirit is excusable in many things—such as machinery,
where rapid progress is made ; but it has been carried
into all departments of life, and too often in the American youth extends to a proverbial disregard for his aged
superiors.   In this general disrespect for aged persons
and things, one of its most painful manifestations is the
placing out of sight of all old furniture.   It is a sorry

thing to go into many of the garrets and sheds of country and other homes, and find piled away there so many articles that were the care and comfort of the former generations of the family. Compare these rejected chairs with those now in use—they are as substantial and easy, and above all, they should be dear to us in memories and associations. We should have more room for memories —we should love the things that our grandfather made, and our grandmother had in daily use. We should keep the old sofa in its appropriate place, where we may rest our weary limbs, and live over the early days of the past, and should we fall into a reverie, and see in our day-dream our good old grandmother, who first folded our little hands to rest on the same old sofa, we should be none the worse for it.

A PACKING BOX CHAIR.

A very comfortable and handsome "chair," shown in figure 147, can be made from an ordinary packing box. The box should be about a foot and a half wide by two feet long, and not more than fourteen inches deep. If deeper it will make the "chair" too high, and so take away much from its ease. A caster should be fastened firmly to each corner; after which the box is ready to cover. Cut from large-flowered chintz as many breadths, sixteen inches deep, as are necessary to go around the sides of the box three times, run them together, make a hem an inch deep around the bottom, and pleat into one and a half inch side pleats. Let the lower edge of the flounce come slightly below the bottom of the box, and lay the extra length over on to the top of the box, where it is fastened with small tacks, so that when the cushion is on the tacks will be covered. To make the cushion, cut two pieces of strong muslin, or partly-worn ticking,

the size of the top of the box, and a piece three inches
deep, which is to be sewed between the top and bottom
of the cushion as for a mattress.   One side should be left
unsewed until the stuffing has been placed in. For this hay
or straw can be used, or worn-out comfortables or quilts.
Enough of whatever is used must be placed in to fill the
cushion tight.   Cut from the chintz a piece the size of
the top of the cushion, and make a strip five inches
deep, and long enough to go once and a half around the

Fig. 147.—A BOX "CHAIR."

cushion.   Gather this strip and sew one side to the piece
of chintz.   Draw over the cushions and sew the other
edge of the puff to the underside.   The cushion can be
tacked firmly to the box along the front, by holding it
up from the back and catching the tacks through the
edge of the puff where it is sewed to the cushion.   For
the back make a pillow four inches less in length than
the box, and not quite as broad as long.   Feathers make
a good stuffing for this, or it may be filled with whatever
is used for the cushion on the box.   Cover the pillow
with chintz, and sew a ruffle of the chintz two inches

wide around it. The ruffle looks better if made double instead of hemmed. Three loops of cord are sewed to the top of the pillow, one at each corner and one in the center, far enough below the edge to keep them from showing above the ruffle, and by these the pillow is hung on nails against the wall back of the covered box.

THE BEST MATCHES.

In buying matches, it is just as well to buy only good ones, and thus compel dealers to keep these only. Some prefer the so-called "parlor matches," on account of their odor, easy ignition, and quick, large flame. But they are not to be recommended for ordinary family use. They are dangerous, liable to burn the fingers, to fly off upon clothing, etc.; if trod on, they will leave a dark, permanent stain, if they do not burn a spot in the carpet or floor, and perchance start a disastrous fire. The brilliant flame is nearly a total waste of expensive chlorate of potash, as it is only the quiet flame of the paraffine on the stick, or of the stick itself, after the igniting sulphur is burned off, that is utilized. The larger amount of phosphorous fumes is quite as unhealthful as the sulphurous odors from ordinary matches. The safest matches are those which will only ignite on the prepared surface of the boxes in which they come; but these are too stationary for general use. The sulphurous fumes from matches are not a serious objection. To the ordinary atmosphere of a room they are disinfectant, and healthful so far as the small quantity from a match has any influence, and, unless purposely or carelessly held near one's face, they are not injurious. The best matches have the following qualities: The stick is of good wood, not easily broken, sufficiently resinous to take fire readily, produce a good-sized flame and hold it against ordinary fair drafts. Test these points

in selecting matches by trying two or three of them.
For ordinary use they should be two or three inches long,
or a little over, but longer for some lamps, chandeliers,
and other special uses; round, smooth, and one-tenth
inch in diameter—ten laid together covering an inch.
The sulphur coating should extend on the stick evenly,
and for only half an inch, so thin as to be scarcely visible,
not in lumps and masses, and no two should stick together. The ignition point is small, round, smooth, extending back uniformly, and less than the diameter of
the stick. Color is non-essential, a matter of taste or
preference.

A USEFUL PAPER HOLDER.

Figure 148 shows a paper holder, so neat in its appear-

ance, that we give an engraving of
it for the benefit of other friends
in the country and elsewhere. It
consists of a thin piece of wood
cut into a pleasing shape, with
a bevelled edge. Narrow slits are
made in four places in the back
piece, for the passage of ribbon, as
shown. The whole is hung to a
hook by the ribbon, which con-
tinues above and from the rear of
the board. The space between the
ribbon and the back furnishes a
place for putting the papers. This
holder is easily made, and may be
of light or dark wood, with plain
or bright colored ribbon, to suit
the taste of the maker.

Fig. 148.—A WALL PAPER
HOLDER.

FARM-HOUSE HAT-RACKS.

A farmer should be proud of his vocation, and when he indulges in anything like ornament, it may well relate to his occupation. This thought occurred to us when we recently saw a hat-rack intended for the hall or entry of a farm-house. It was imported, and essentially English in every detail. Those who are fond of making such things in the work-shop will be glad of this hint and improve upon and Americanize it. The basis of the hat-rack is a harrow, about two and a half or three feet square, made of horizontal bars, crossing one another at right angles, as in a common harrow. The harrow teeth serve as pins for hats and coats. In the center is a diamond-shaped mirror. At the bottom is a double-tree and two single-trees, which may be merely for ornament or use. Above are placed, crossing behind the harrow, the handles showing below, a scythe and a fork, while between them is a sickle, an implement rarely used by us at present. This rack is intended to be hung against the wall ; another is so constructed as to stand by itself. The handles of a rake, a fork, and a flail, are placed to form a tripod, and held together at the point of crossing by a stout metallic band. A sickle is added for ornament. There are pins in the central band upon which to hang garments, etc., while hooks for the same purpose are placed here and there on the handles, and even upon the flail itself. The wood-work in these racks is ash, finished in oil or some very light varnish. The blades of scythes and sickles are apparently of silvered sheet copper. The finest kind of tin plate, properly polished, would answer about as well. Forms made of stiff paste-board, or thin, light wood, and neatly covered with the best tin foil (it may be fastened on with flour paste) might be better than tin. The stronger metal work, such as harrow teeth, rings, hooks, etc., are

of iron, nickel-plated.   Those who have not the facilities
for getting plating done, will find that if the iron hook
is covered with a good black varnish, it will look almost
as well as if plated.

SUPPORTS FOR SHOVEL AND TONGS.

Figure 149 shows a shovel and tongs support in rustic
work, easily made by any ingenious person.   In a support

Fig. 149.—RUSTIC SUPPORT.

of this kind the base should be as a shallow box to contain stones or pieces of old iron in order to give sufficient
weight and stability.   The base may be stained with
umber and varnished, or covered with oil-cloth with a
piece of zinc on the upper side for the irons to rest on.

DECORATIVE ART.

Decorative art has been defined as the beautifying of useful things. But to the enthusiastic decorator, every-thing of pleasing effect has its use, if it be only to delight the eye. A piece of bright color, laid by childish hands against a bare and sombre wall, if it is in harmony with its surroundings, and relieves the monotony of a dull and cheerless surface, becomes at once a thing of use. Noth-

Fig. 150.—CARVED WALL-POCKET.

ing that renders home attractive, or upon which the eye may fall with pleasure, is so small and mean as to be de-spised. While we counsel against the purchase of poor pictures, misshapen statuettes, and the thousand and one cheap ornaments, we would suggest the use of the saw, the chisel, the paint-brush and the needle. A panel painted by inexperienced fingers, however weakly, is preferable to the colored lithograph or poor chromo, and a carving but roughly done by hand, is infinitely more desirable than the veneered and highly glazed surface of the cheap wood-work. The home-made article will at least have the value of originality, and will show care and study, if not good taste. None need despair of some success, and while all may not be able to produce a work valuable for its artistic merits alone, yet each may so

Fig. 151.—A CARVED BRACKET.

adorn and beautify some article of use that it may become as valuable for its ornamental qualities as for its usefulness. Above all, let it be noted that beauty does not depend upon costliness of material, but rather upon a harmonious combination of effects, and the adaptiveness of each article for the place assigned to it. Save every bright colored scrap that by bare possibility even may be of use ; preserve bits of broken ornaments, old legs of chairs, if they are firm and solid, broken moldings, and the time may come when you will need just such a piece as you now despise, and will go gladly to the store-house to find it. First in importance in decorative art may be placed wood carving. We give two articles usually chosen by the inexperienced as most easy of construction, and requiring but little ornamentation, viz., the Wall-Pocket and the Bracket.

The wall-pocket (figure 150) is much the simpler and is very easily put together. Half-inch boards will be re-

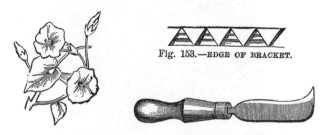

Fig. 153.—EDGE OF BRACKET.

Fig. 152.—DESIGN FOR CARVING.   Fig. 154.—KNIFE.

quired for these—a little heavier for the shelf of the bracket and its support—the wood chosen to be at the option or convenience of the worker. Black-walnut is always desirable, as being most easily worked and the most satisfactory when finished. Cherry is handsome— of a rich, deep red when oiled, but tough and hard to work, and apt to crumble under the tool. Oak should never be attempted by the inexperienced. For economy, pine or any other cheap wood may be used, and stained after carving, but this is not desirable when it can be avoided. Ebonized wood is, however, very effective when an incised pattern only is desired, the pattern to be marked off with gilt or touches of paper—with the

point of the carving-knife held straight down, cut
all around the edge of the pattern; then sloping the knife
a little cut around once again, thus removing a narrow slice of wood, which will leave the pattern quite dis-
tinct and clear, care being taken that the edges of the

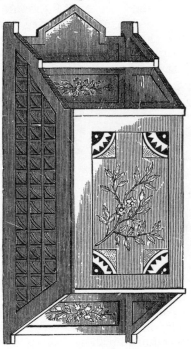

Fig. 155.—A HANGING CARVED CABINET.

leaves are sharp, and that the sloping cut is taken from
the back-ground and not from the pattern. All this
may be done with a V-chisel or dividing tool, but it is a
dangerous instrument in the hands of the novice, and
one slip may ruin all. The veining of the leaves is done
with a little instrument called a veining tool, which must
be handled carefully, as an unlucky slip will make a cut

that can not be repaired. A line should be drawn all around the wall-pocket or bracket about one-quarter of an inch from the edge, and cut away with the knife as above described, thus leaving a border or frame for the carved picture already made. Then with a stamping or fretting tool roughen the back ground, leaving the pattern smooth, and stamp carefully between the leaves and stems. This is a very simple process, and is done by holding the stamp in the left hand and striking it a quick blow with a mallet, the impression of the pattern on the under side of the stamping tool being left in the wood.

The necessary tools required for this work are gouges of four different sizes, and as it will be found that the round bladed or U-shaped gouge will be equally as necessary as the flat, it will be best to get four of each, and chisels, both straight and bent, with edges varying from the smallest procurable to an inch in width. A knife of the shape in figure 154 will be found an absolute necessity. An oil-stone is most suitable for repairing edges dulled by work, but a small fine grind-stone should be kept at hand for the breaks that will occur; it must be used very carefully.

Fig. 156.
SIDE ORNAMENT.

Figure 155 is a design for a hanging cabinet which will be useful, as well as ornamental. It may be black-walnut, oak, or ash. It is exceedingly simple in construction, and will bear much elaborate ornamentation, upon which, indeed, its beauty will mainly depend. The wood-carver should have thoroughly understood ideas before attempting to put them into execution, since mistakes cannot be rectified and regrets over errors in composition will prove unavailing when seen too late.

It is always advisable for the student to go to Nature for designs, where there is an endless variety of admirable subjects for the chisel ; skill and ingenuity in adapting such things as may appear suitable will soon be acquired. Leaves and flowers are the most easily represented, and while we may not in wood reproduce the loveliness of tint or delicacy of texture, we may very faithfully give the grace of outline, the tender curves of the flower, and the bolder sweep of leaf. Birds are especially showy and ornamental, requiring but little of the finer work ; animals of all kinds, and even the human figure, may be adapted to the purpose of our ornamentation. It is best to start out with a well formed idea in view, and carry it faithfully throughout the whole work, otherwise the effect may be fragmentary and not wholly satisfactory. Scroll-hinges, nickel-plated, add greatly to effect where hinges are required, and may be procured of any size. The design for ornamenting the door, or other parts of the cabinet, may be furnished according to the worker's own taste, in bold relief or the more easily executed incised work ; in the former case, the wood of the panel should be thick, according to the depth of the cutting, as the gluing on of extra thickness is not to be recommended. The spray of apple blossoms on the door of the cabinet is merely a suggestion, but might be carefully handled in low relief, especially if copied from nature, so as to produce an exquisite effect. Figure 156 is a figure which may be used for a side ornament.

HINTS ON USING BENZINE.

Benzine dissolves fats and oils, resins, varnishes, paint, etc., so readily, that it is largely used for the purpose of cleaning clothing and other fabrics. It is within the recollection of many that benzine was once rather costly, and could only be purchased in small bottles at a high price. Now it is cheap; the makers of kerosene produce so much more benzine than there is a demand for, that, at wholesale at least, it bears but a nominal price. Benzine, in careless hands, is a very dangerous article, and no one should use it without understanding its properties, that accidents may be guarded against. It boils at one hundred and forty degrees Fahrenheit, and at all ordinary temperatures rapidly evaporates. When this vapor is mingled with the air, the two form a mixture which, in contact with a flame, will explode violently. The vapor of benzine, when not mixed with air to form an explosive mixture, will readily take fire and burn rapidly. A bottle partly filled, in a warm room, will give off the vapor so freely, that it will take fire even when at a distance of several inches from a lamp. In working with benzine, always use it by daylight, and in a room without a fire, or so far from a fire that there can be no danger. These facts can not be too thoroughly impressed upon all who have occasion to use this liquid for any purpose. In using benzine and other solvents for removing grease or other spots from fabrics, a mere wetting often is given, and after the benzine has evaporated, the place looks worse than before. By applying a little benzine, the grease or other substance is dissolved, and this solution spreads to the surrounding portions of the cloth and the evil is increased. We must use the liquid in such a manner as to dissolve the grease and then to carry away the solution—we must, in fact, wash out the spot with benzine. To do this, it is not necessary to immerse the article or a large portion of it. In removing a spot, first fold some old woollen cloths, or even porous newspapers, to form a thick pad. Place this pad under the article, and wet the spot with benzine. Use a sponge or a roll of woollen cloth, and rub the spot, adding more benzine as it is taken up by the pad below.   In this manner the benzine holding the grease, etc., in solution, is absorbed by the pad, and the solution is washed out of the cloth by successive quantities of benzine, to be also carried down into the pad. Success depends upon using sufficient benzine ; it is cheap, and one need not be sparing of it. Gloves are cleaned by immersing them in benzine in a wide-mouthed glass-stoppered bottle.   The gloves are shaken up with the liquid for a few minutes, taken out, squeezed, and hung under a chimney to dry. If any spots are left, these are rubbed with a rag wet with benzine.   If the gloves retain any odor, they are placed in a plate, covered by another, and the whole set upon a kettle of boiling water.   The heat will soon drive off the odor.

RACK FOR NEWSPAPERS.

In a family where a number of papers are taken it is almost a necessity to have some accessible place besides

Fig. 157.—RACK FOR NEWSPAPERS.

the table in which to keep them.   A rack like the one given in figure 157 can be hung beside the table, or on an out-of-the-way bit of wall space, and answers the purpose admirably. It is easily made of heavy card-board. Cut two pieces eighteen inches long and twelve inches wide for the back, and two pieces the same length, and ten inches wide, for the front. The back pieces are covered with gray linen, and sewed or bound together. The inner piece of the front is also faced with linen. The outside piece is covered with bronze-green felt, with corners of a darker shade, worked on with feather stitch in black silk floss. The bands are of darker shade, worked with bright colored silks in various hues. The band is fastened on the front with "blind stitch." The long stitches which go across from one edge of the band to the other are of bright yellow brown; the shorter stitches which cross them are of dark red and light blue, and the stitches which extend outwards from the edge of the band are of black and pink silk. The bands are sewed on before the felt is attached to the paste-board. After the two front pieces are fitted together, the back and front are sewed together along the bottom, and a cord is attached to the front piece near the top, taken through two holes in the back, and fastened. Three brass rings are very firmly sewed to the upper edge of the back, by which the rack is hung against the wall.

A very pretty rack can be made by using linen throughout, omitting the corner-pieces, and making the bands of velvet, of knot-work, or of canvas, worked with bright wool and silk. The shape may be changed by slightly rounding the upper corners of the front, or both the front and back.

HOME-MADE FRAMES FOR PICTURES.

Pictures and engravings that one does not permanently frame may be temporarily placed upon the wall by the use of narrow strips of wood covered with velvet. The

8

strips should be long enough to extend an inch beyond
the sides of the picture, and after they have been placed
over the picture, as shown in figure 158, they are
fastened to the wall by brass-headed tacks at each end.
To cover the strips cut a piece of velvet a little longer
and wider than the length and width of the strip, and

Fig. 158.—STRIPS FOR HOLDING PICTURES.

draw it tightly over it by taking stitches from edge to
edge of the velvet on the wrong side, being careful to
make the corners sharp and neat.   The size of the strips
depends on the size of the picture.   For a small picture,
about five by seven, or the size of a large photograph,
they need not be more than half or a third of an inch
wide, while for a picture four or five times that size, they
should be an inch and a half or two inches wide.   For
small pictures pieces of cigar boxes answer the purpose

well, and for large ones a lath, all the better if planed, does nicely. By using long strips, six or eight photographs can be placed side by side with very good effect. This is also a good way to arrange pictures in the nursery or a child's-room, where the decorations are frequently changed. They do not have the unfinished look of an unframed picture.

FROST-BITES AND CHILBLAINS.

Probably no other forms of accident or injury come upon us so unexpectedly as those due to excessive cold. As a general thing we are not aware that a part is being frozen until the mischief is already done. This is due to the fact that one of the effects of severe cold is to destroy the sensitiveness of the parts exposed. Surgeons make use of this fact in small operations, and cool the parts by artificial cold. The ears, the nose, sometimes the cheeks, and the hands and feet are the parts most liable to be frozen. One of the first effects of freezing is to stop the circulation of the blood, and any part in which the circulation is checked by other means, is all the more likely to be frozen. The old-fashioned skates, held on by numerous tight straps across the feet, are dangerous on this account; to keep them in place, the straps are drawn so tightly as to impede the circulation in the feet, and frost-bitten feet are often the consequence. Though the operation of freezing is painless, a sudden thawing is attended with inflammation and great pain. The thawing should be very slow, in order that the circulation in the parts may be restored gradually. For this reason it is advised to rub the frozen parts with snow, or in the absence of that, with water made as cold as possible with ice. It is said that in Russia, when one observes that another's nose or face is being frozen, it is an act of com-

mon politeness to catch up a handful of snow and apply
it to the face of the unfortunate, even if he is a perfect
stranger. In cases of severe freezing, besides gradual
thawing by the use of snow or ice, a physician should be
called, as it may be that proper precautions are needed to
prevent mortification of the parts. It is not necessary for
the feet to be actually frozen to produce chilblains. The
term frost-bitten is usually applied to such cases. Children
often suffer greatly from getting their feet very cold, and
then going to the fire to warm them. The circulation is
disturbed, and the parts remain exceedingly sensitive to
future changes of cold and heat. Chilblains vary from a
slight inflammation, to severe cases in which the skin
breaks, and even ulcers are formed. Of course such cases
require professional treatment. To allay the intense itching and pain of ordinary chilblains, a great number of
applications have been used. An ounce of sulphate of
zinc (white vitriol), in a pint of water, or an ounce of sal
ammoniac dissolved in half a pint each of vinegar and
alcohol are among the washes often used. It is stated on
good authority, though we have not had occasion to try
it, that the application of ordinary kerosene oil is very
efficacious in allaying the itching and pain.

FLOWER BOX, WITH SUPPORTS.

Flowers in pots do not, as a rule, have room enough to
expand their roots properly ; we have had more success
with flowers grown in boxes of the shape given in figure 159. This box is convenient for window-garden-
ing, or can be used in the summer for plants generally
set into pots. Some of the finest geraniums we ever
raised during the winter months were grown in such a
box. It is made of inch pine, the bottom being common
rough stuff of that thickness, and the sides of planed

material. It is thirty inches long and twelve inches wide, the sides being four inches high. It should be screwed together, to prevent the moisture in the soil from drawing the joints apart, which is often the case when

Fig. 159.—A FLOWER BOX.

nails are used. In each corner, neat, nicely planed oak or hickory pieces, one inch square, are securely fastened, the pieces being about twelve or fifteen inches high; to these are attached stout cords, to keep the branches of the plant within bounds. The box can be painted, stained, or varnished on the outside, as may be desired by the owner.

FAN COVER FOR FLOWER POT.

A green, thrifty, growing plant, even in a common pot, is in itself an ornament to any room, but some kind

Fig. 160.—COVER FOR FLOWER POT.

of a cover to set on over the plain pot, is often an addition that does much to increase its beauty. Very pretty covers can be made out of the Japanese fans which can be so cheaply bought. Remove the fastening which holds the sticks together at the bottom, and cut them off close to the lower edge of the fan. Make two holes in the sticks at each side of the fan, one an inch from the upper edge, and the other the same distance from the

lower. Run a fine thread through each fold of the fan at the top and bottom, and fasten at each end after drawing it up to the right size to fit around the pot it is to cover. If very fine thread is used, and small stitches taken, they will show but little. Run a coarser thread through the holes in the sticks, and fasten the cover on the pot by running the thread through the

Fig. 161.—POT WITH COVER.

opposite holes and tying it. It is well to select the fan with some regard to the color of the flowers of the plants it is to be near. For the cover of a pot holding a geranium with bright scarlet flowers, a fan with a gray ground, covered with figures in which black, blue and gilt predominate, would look best, but for a rose geranium or an ivy, a bright colored fan could be used with good effect.

EASILY MADE HANGING BASKETS.

A basket for plants is of less consequence than its contents; if costly, the beauty of the plants should conceal that of the receptacle, and if homely, the plant will exalt it, and make the whole beautiful. Figure 162 shows a simple easily made hanging-basket. Almost any straight sticks or twigs, all the better if they have a rough bark, are laid up in cob-house style. Such a basket is best put together with bits of strong wire at the corners. Holes are bored, the wires passed through, making a twist or knot below, and above twisting to form an eye to serve to attach the cord or chain by which to hang it. Of course similar strips, or even pieces of lath, should be used for the bottom. Such a basket is best lined with the moss that is found growing at the base of

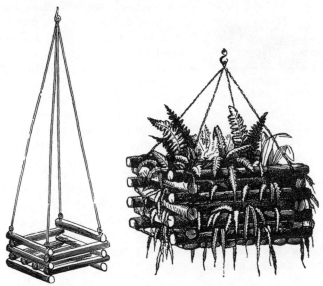

Fig. 162.—A SIMPLE HANG-
ING BASKET.

Fig. 163.—A HANGING BASKET FILLED
WITH PLANTS.

trees in moist woods; this can be pulled off in large sheets, and is easily fitted to the interior of such a basket. While it keeps the soil in place, it allows ferns and other plants to grow through it. Figure 163 shows a similar basket filled with common wild ferns, but it will answer equally well for exotics. The winter is the time in which to prepare such baskets for summer use on the veranda. Though these examples are square, it is equally easy to make six-sided baskets of similar materials. A window-box may be easily constructed in the same manner, to be furnished with a zinc lining.

A NEAT, RUSTIC FLOWER STAND.

Figure 164 shows how a crotched stick, such as any one can find in the forest, may be turned to good service in making a stand for holding a pot of window plants. The three branches, serving as legs of the tripod, should come from the main trunk at nearly the same point, and be about equally distant from each other at their lower ends. The size, both as regards hight and thickness, of the trunk and legs, will be determined by the space allowed for the stand, the size of the pot it is desired to hold, etc. The construction of this easily and quickly made rustic stand is made clear by the accompanying engraving.

Fig. 164.—FLOWER STAND.

CANARY BIRDS.

Many questions are asked about the Canary Birds especially as to care, breeding, etc. This pretty little captive bird—and its prison is a happy one, or should be made so —gets its common name from the Canary Isles, where it abounds in its wild state, and is clothed in a gray or brown plumage, quite in contrast with the white, yellow, and green of the domesticated varieties. The Canary birds have long been esteemed for their beauty and melody, and were domesticated in Europe nearly three centuries ago, where, at the present time, they are bred on an extensive scale, especially in France and Germany, from which countries we import them by the tens of thousands. The Canary-bird trade is vastly greater than would be supposed by those who have not looked into the subject. In England there have been annual shows—and what beautiful shows they must be!—for the last half century, at which large prizes have been awarded among the different varieties, which are reckoned up by dozens. So far as looks are concerned, a bird is valued according to the purity of its coloring, or if mixed, in proportion as the markings are regular. A mottled or spotted bird is not held in much esteem, while one which is a pure yellow, or a yellow with black wings and tail, is greatly prized. But above the color is the song; and in the choice of a bird it is best to observe the rule, "Sacrifice color to accomplishment." Nature seldom unites rare beauty and great accomplishments. A person should not reject a sweet singer because its tail feathers are gone; they will soon come out; but this can not be said of the voice where it is wanting. Some estimate a bird's value by the loudness of the voice; we prefer the softer—and we think sweeter—tones, in fact, have almost been incensed by the noise which some birds will make when they sing.

There are many different styles of cages, but none should sacrifice the comfort of the bird or endanger its life. The large wooden frame cages are fast passing out of use, and are superseded by those made entirely of metal, which are neater, lighter, easier cleaned, and less liable to harbor insects. The wires, against which a bird will often pick more or less, should never be coated with paint, as it may cause its death. Ample provision should be made for food and water within the cages, and there should be a proper arrangement for hanging it up—a hook, or a stout ring, is better to hang it by than a ribbon, which in time will wear out, when the cage and contents may have a fall. Perches and a swing will of course be provided. Canaries are very fond of a bath, and should be given water for one nearly every day. The tub should be removed when the bath is over. To see the little fellow enjoy the splashing and fluttering, is worth all the trouble. Above all things in the keeping of birds, neatness is of the greatest importance. They need attention every day. If the bird is " too much of a trouble," then do not keep it a day. Birds are very tender things, and as such are very susceptible to treatment, good or bad. They should have a plenty of air and light, but not the dazzling sunshine. A bird should not be out-of-doors when the air is at all chilly ; and in winter is is cruel to leave it in a room in which the temperature goes down to freezing or below.

What shall we feed our birds ? is a question frequently asked, and it is an important one, as their health depends largely upon their food. Do not dose them with sweetmeats ; their systems demand a plain diet. The natural food of the Canaries is seeds and green herbage, and a mixture of rape, canary, and hemp seed, together with chickweed, cress, cabbage, etc., is found to be the most healthful. A cuttle-fish bone (sold at the drug stores) hung in the cage will furnish the lime they need, and which they find in the wild state.

Perhaps the most important point is to know what to do when the bird is sick. With proper care they seldom sicken, but sometimes illness is unavoidable. Birds will, without any apparent reason, take colds, followed by sneezing and hoarseness. For this a bit of liquorice, placed in the drinking water, proves beneficial. In case of loss of appetite, shedding of feathers, and general decline, a plenty of water-cress is valuable. Young birds are frequently troubled with "gapes," and should have an abundance of green food and be kept in a warm place. Canaries that are not properly cared for will be infested with lice, for which some anise-seed mixed with the gravel on the floor is a preventive. Epilepsy is caused by too rich food ; the cure is in quiet and a simpler diet. In cases of diarrhœa put a rusty nail in the drinking water and chalk, broken fine, on the floor, omitting all green food. A bird well cared for—and the care is by no means great—is a cheerful and cheering companion. If one loves such a pet—and most people do—the care is more than repaid in bright plumage, graceful actions, and sweet music of these little birds.

SWEET POTATO VINE FOR THE WINDOW.

The sweet potato vine is not so often used as an ornamental plant, as it would be, were the beauty of its dark green foliage generally known. It is very easily managed, being usually grown in water, though it may be set in earth in a pot. A hyacinth-glass, or other glass, or whatever may be the most convenient vessel to hold the water, may be used, and a good, sound sweet potato selected, of such size that it will rest upon the edge of the vessel, with its lower part just touching the water. It requires a considerable heat to start it, and should be set in a warm place, where it will have a temperature of seventy-five or eighty degrees. Light is not needed until the shoots have started, but when growth has begun, then give it a sunny place. If many shoots start, remove all but three or four of the strongest, or, if the vine is to be trained to run up over the window, two will be better than more. Grown in a vase set upon a bracket, as shown in figure 165, and the branches allowed to fall down gracefully, it makes a charming ornament ; in this case a number of small and slender shoots are preferable to a few large ones, and several buds may be allowed to

Fig. 165.—SWEET POTATO VINE.

grow. All the care needed is to add water, which, when the leaves are numerous, will be taken up and evaporated rapidly.

SUGGESTIONS ABOUT CARPET-SWEEPING.

Sweeping is a good exercise if you can avoid raising a dust. But if you are in need of vigorous exercise of that kind, get a hoe and betake yourself to the potato-patch or corn-field. Sweep carpets gently. Even a rag carpet should be treated with consideration. A severe digging with a stiff broom wears the warp and scrapes out the lint of the rags quite needlessly. Not long ago we heard a woman say that a very stiff broom was needed for sweeping a Brussels carpet. A carpet-sweeper is the best thing for this purpose. It does the work easily and well, and saves dust. A brush of hair and dust-pan are good to use for the nicest carpets, but their use is too laborious for recommendation to a busy house-keeper. If a common broom-corn broom must be used for Brussels, it should be fine, soft, light, and clean. To sweep up threads, ravelings, and other fine litter, many persons wet the broom in clean tepid water, shaking out the water before sweeping with it, just keeping the broom moist enough to wipe up the dust and threads, rinsing in clear water and shaking it frequently as the work progresses. Brussels carpets are not suitable for rooms where sewing and baby-culture are going forward. In providing carpets for any room, reason would dictate that they be such as may easily be kept clean ; not so dark as to show every dust and thread, nor so light as to be very easily soiled— something which will either let the dust sift through or retain it on the surface, rather than in the carpet itself, when to be used in rooms where dust is made.

CARE OF CARPETS.

To make sweeping an easy task, get carpets of a kind that are easily swept, then save them from unnecessary litter by care about scattering fine chips or crumbs of wood, cloth, paper, or food. Eating should be done in rooms easily cleaned, with carpets of oil-cloth, or similar material, or with bare floors, or with a linen crumb-cloth spread upon the carpet underneath the table. Children should not be allowed to run about the house with pieces of food in their hands. If their food is not all taken at the table, the child should be obliged to sit still some-where, catching its crumbs upon a napkin, bib, or apron, instead of dropping them upon the floor. Children who learn "to save mamma trouble," and so get at least a smile of gratitude from her for their thoughtfulness, are far happier than those who are not trained to care, but are allowed to make themselves a general nuisance among orderly people. If they wish to whittle, or to cut paper or "dolly things" in your best rooms, you need not neces-sarily refuse them. Spread a large cloth or newspaper down, to catch the chips or clippings, and see that it is safely emptied so soon as the child's work is done. Grown-up people are sometimes very annoying, because of their lack of this kind of early training. They pull flowers to pieces in your parlors, whittle on your smoothly-shaven lawn, scatter fruit peelings and cigar stumps about the yard, scribble on the covers of your magazines and margins of newspapers, and scratch matches on the walls of the house, or leave disagreeable marks of some kind in every possible place.

After the carpet and the care, next comes the broom— soft and limber, and not too large and heavy. We always send for light brooms now, having found how much more strength it uses up to wield a large and heavy broom. Besides, except for scrubbing, we want a broom to use gently. A short, quick stroke takes all the dust along before it, and does not send it flying all over the shelves, pictures, etc., so that much that has been stirred up and set flying about, settles back over the carpet again. Keep the dust low, sweeping just hard enough to move it quickly

along before the broom.   If there is a very dusty room to
sweep, cover the furniture, or that which is upholstered,
and the shelves and tables with books or small articles
upon them, and afterwards shake the covers out of doors.

WINDOW SHELVES FOR PLANTS.

If one has window shelves for plants, it is convenient
to have them so arranged that the plants may receive the
greatest possible benefit from the light in the daytime,
without incurring the risk of freezing at night.   To accomplish this, take two of the castings
used to hold up the ends of curtain rollers,
figure 166, and fasten them on the inside
window casing at the desired hight.   For
the shelf, use half-inch stuff, cutting it
the shape shown in figure 167.   The width
at the widest part may be five or six
inches; at the ends one inch.   Bore
gimlet holes lengthwise into the narrow
ends as indicated by the dotted lines,

Fig. 166.—THE
BRACKET.

slip the shelf between the castings, and put a picture
nail through the hole in each casting, and into the
gimlet hole in the corresponding end of the shelf.
Insert a screw-hook in the ceiling above, directly over a
point half way between the short edge of the shelf when
turned toward the glass, and the same edge when turned

Fig. 167.—THE WINDOW SHELF.

toward the apartment.   From this hook No. 10 wires
descend, and are hooked upon wood-screws in the edge of
the short side, the shelf itself being thus supported in a
horizontal position, whether turned in or out.   If other

shelves are required, they may be put between castings
fastened lower on the casings, and be supported horizon-
tally by a wire depending from the edge of the upper
shelf.   The advantage of the arrangement is that, in addition to the higher temperature secured for the plants

Fig. 168.—THE SHELF IN POSITION.

by the turning of the shelf, the window curtain can be
conveniently interposed between the glass and the shelf
at night.   If a wider shelf is desired, a suitable block
may first be attached to the casing, and the casting
screwed to that; or, if the castings are not at hand, a

bracket-like block may be used instead. Care should be taken to have the shelf fill the space between the end supports, as in this way it will be stronger, and the whole affair should be as light as is consistent with necessary strength.

PLANT-SHELVES IN WINDOWS.

Those who keep window-plants will find that the fol-

Fig. 169.—PLANT SHELVES IN WINDOW.

lowing plan for attaching shelves to the windows will be useful in many cases, though, of course, its applicability

will depend much upon the manner in which the house
is built.   The movable strip, or "stop," which holds the
sash in place, is taken out, and in its place is put one an
an inch thick, and four or five inches wide, or as wide as
the window casing will allow, as shown in figure 169,
There are, of course, two of these, and in each is a series
of grooves or "gains," intended to admit the ends of the
shelves.   To make this plain an enlarged portion is

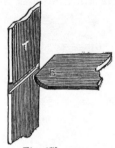

Fig. 170.—SHELF.   Fig. 171.—BRACKET.

shown in figure 170.   By rounding the corners of the
shelves, those for the larger pots may be six or seven
inches wide, while the side strip which supports them is
only four inches wide.   Figure 169 shows a window thus
furnished.   When the shelves are no longer required, the
side-pieces may be taken out and the "stops" returned,
and no part of the window-frame will have been marred
or injured in any way.   Where it is not practicable to
remove the "stops," and substitute side-pieces, then the
shelves may be supported on brackets, of the form shown
in figure 171.   Any blacksmith can make these of a piece
of nail-rod ; they should be furnished with holes for
screws, by which they can be attached to the window-
frames, and there should also be a hole at P, through
which to pass a screw from below into the bottom of the
shelf, to hold it firm.—This form of bracket will answer
to support a window-box, which is by many window-gar-

deners preferred to pots. Any rough box, of a length to
suit the window, and about six inches high and wide,
will answer. Have the tinman make a zinc lining to fit,
and high enough to turn over the edge of the box, so
that no earth may get between the box and the lining.
The outside of the box may be covered to suit the fancy;
strips of bark, or split twigs, will give a pleasant rustic
effect, or it may be covered with a bit of floor oil-cloth,
with a molding on the edges. A box covered with oil-
cloth of a mechanical pattern has every appearance of an
expensive tile-covered box. Recollect that a box of this
kind is very heavy when filled, and the brackets and
their fastening must be correspondingly strong.

DIPHTHERIA—WHAT TO DO.

While we are opposed to frequent medication for every
little ailing, we think that every mother should under-
stand the general laws of health, and sufficient of diseases
to know when it is safe for her to apply some simple
remedy, and when the case is sufficiently grave to make
it necessary to call in medical aid at once. In many cases
the success of the physician depends upon his being called
at once, while it is too often the case that he is not sent
for until all the medical knowledge of the parents and
neighbors is exhausted, and the patient still grows worse.
There is no disease in which immediate aid is more im-
peratively demanded than diphtheria. It is eminently
contagious, and every precaution should be taken to prevent its being communicated from one to another. When
the disease prevails in a locality, children should be kept
as much as possible from contact with others, and as persons in whom it has not manifested itself, are able to communicate the disease, all fondling of children, and "kiss-
ing the baby" by callers, should be avoided. Before there

is any difficulty of breathing, there is a constant pain at the sides of the throat, and this is accompanied by very fetid breath, and the appearance of whitish spots upon the sides of the throat (fauces), the back part of the throat, or the roof of the mouth, is an indication sufficiently strong to call for medical examination at once. The remedies employed by physicians are various, but none is so generally used, and none have been found, if used in time, more reliable than the chlorate of potash. While we do not advise any parent to assume the responsibility of treating so grave a disease as diphtheria, we may suggest how they can essentially aid the physician, and this is of especial importance to those who live at a long distance from the doctor, and where many hours must pass before he can arrive, for in this disease hours are of great importance. Chlorate of potash, to be had at all drug stores, is a salt in small, white, scale-like crystals, which are not very soluble in water. It may be kept on hand in the form of crystals, or when the disease is prevalent in the neighborhood, it may be well to keep a solution ready for use. It takes about sixteen parts of cold water to dissolve one part of the chlorate, and it is to be used in a saturated solution. To prepare this, it is only necessary to add to water more of the chlorate than it will dissolve. Half an ounce placed into a four-ounce vial of water, will be about twice as much as the water will dissolve. As long as any remains undissolved, the solution is known to be saturated —i. e., the water can take up no more. If the ordinary water is hard, use rain water. Upon the appearance of symptoms which seem to indicate diphtheria, a dose of this may be given every hour, a teaspoonful for a child three years and older, and half a teaspoonful to those under three. It is to be given undiluted, and without any sweetening or other admixture, as its taste is not very unpleasant. Drink of any kind should not be given for some minutes after a dose, as it is desirable that the solution should remain in contact with the surfaces of the throat and mouth as long as possible. Children old enough to gargle the throat, may take the dose every hour, and every half hour use the same as a gargle. This is only intended to aid the physician's treatment, and is advised only for cases in which some hours must elapse before they can be attended. When the doctor comes, tell him exactly what has been done, and how many doses have been given. Those situated quite beyond the reach of medical aid, cannot do better than continue the administration of the solution every hour, day and night, until the spots in the throat begin to disappear, when their frequency may be diminished to two, and later to three hours, giving all the while the most nourishing food. This advice has the sanction of the most eminent medical authorities, but we repeat, it is only to be followed until the doctor comes, and at the first appearance of diphtheria, or what seems to be that, lose no time, but send for medical aid at once.

WATER OF AMMONIA, OR SPIRITS OF HARTSHORN.

The water of ammonia is of great utility in the household. This is a solution of ammonia gas in water. Ammonia is formed when animal matters are distilled in a certain manner ; the early chemists produced it from the horns of the deer or hart, and as they regarded everything that was distilled as a "spirit," they called this Spirits of Hartshorn. The gas, ammonia, is invisible, but we can readily recognize it by its strong and pungent odor. One of its peculiarities is, the readiness with which it dissolves in water. At ordinary temperatures, water will dissolve over six hundred times its own bulk of the gas. The liquid sold by the druggists as spirits of hartshorn, is merely a solution of this gas in water, hence the more accurate name for it is water of ammonia. Two kinds are kept in the shops, one three times as strong as the other. If simply water of ammonia is asked for, the weaker kind is given ; to procure the other, the "strong" must be designated. To keep it, the bottle must be closed by a well-fitting glass stopper which is waxed, or by a rubber one, as it soon destroys a cork. When applied to the skin, ammonia is a powerful stimulant, and the strong solution will blister very promptly. It is usually applied externally in the form of a liniment. If one part of ordinary water of ammonia be mixed with two parts of olive oil, they form a liquid soap which is known as volatile liniment, and used wherever the stimulant action of ammonia is needed, especially in the sore throats of children.

Being strongly alkaline, it is useful to neutralize acids, and when strong acids are spilled upon clothing or other fabrics, an immediate application of ammonia may arrest their destructive action. When black fabrics are discolored by most acids, ammonia will restore the color. The readiness with which it combines with oil and grease of all kinds, makes it most serviceable in removing such articles from the clothing. Applied to a grease spot, it forms at once a soap with the oil or fat, which may then be washed out. Unless the application be followed by washing with water, it will do little or no good. A mixture of equal parts of water of ammonia and alcohol forms one of the best liquids for cleaning woollen clothing, there being few spots or stains which water will not remove, that will not be dissolved by the ammonia or the alcohol. In using this, apply it well to the spot, and then wash the place with a sponge and warm water. There is no way in which hair brushes and combs, especially fine ones, can be kept in good order so easily, as by an occasional washing in water (blood warm), to which enough water of ammonia has been added to make it smell rather strongly. A washing in this at once cleanses a soiled hair brush and makes it look as bright and as good as new.

RUSTIC WINDOW BOXES.

Many persons would have flowers in their rooms if it were not for the trouble entailed by a number of pots. The earth in pots soon dries out and separates, and frequent watering, with its attendant drip and "muss," makes the care of them a task. When a cold snap comes

Fig. 172.—BOX COVERED WITH CEDAR STICKS.

on it is often necessary, especially in country houses, to remove the plants to some warmer quarter, and the carrying about of a dozen or two pots is no light task. Then pots of themselves are undeniably unsightly, unless one buys very expensive ones ; and if they are not filled with plants that are particularly attractive, the collection as a whole, pots and plants, is not altogether satisfactory as an ornament to the dwelling. All of these objections may be overcome by the use of window-boxes. The earth does not dry out rapidly; if the plants must be moved they can all be lifted at once ; the box can be made of a pleasing appearance and an ornament in itself should the plants not be especially attractive, or even if it contained no plants at all. In figures 172 to 174, are given three rustic window boxes ; the foundation in all cases is a box of sound pine, which need not of necessity be planed. The size of the box should have reference to that of the window. Some windows have sills broad enough to hold the box, but where this is not the case it may rest upon a couple of brackets screwed to the wall. Wooden brackets may be used, or cast-iron ones, which may be had at a cheap rate at the large hardware stores. The box should be thoroughly nailed, and strong in its make. In figure 172 cedar sticks, straight and of the same size, are split in halves, the bark left on, and firmly nailed to the box. In figure 173 is shown a box, covered with some well-marked bark ; in the case of the one figured that of the white-wood or tulip-tree, common throughout all the Western States, is used. Figure 174 shows a more elaborate style, which in reality is more effective than can be shown in the engraving. The ornamentation here is done with halved sticks, those shown light being of white birch, the silvery bark of which

Fig. 173.—BOX COVERED WITH BARK.

is in strong contrast with the darker pieces, which are apparently laurel or some dark-barked wood. In this last case the wood was varnished, which we do not consider an improvement. Either of these boxes is of a most pleasing exterior, and while it would not seem out of place in the most elegant parlor, would grace and add an air of refinement to the humblest kitchen. So much for the outside of the box, which any one who really sets herself about it can accomplish without difficulty.   As to the inside : If you wish to do the best thing, get a pan of sheet zinc or galvanized iron made to exactly fit it.   If this expense should not be warranted, use the box without it, but in case of over-watering it may drip, and if not thoroughly and carefully nailed the sides may warp ; but a little foresight will avoid these difficulties.   A good

Fig. 174.—BOX WITH MOSAIC WORK.

mechanic can make a box quite water-tight by putting thick white-lead or a strip of paper dipped in tar between the joints before nailing.   Now, to fill it, lay in the bottom—whether it has a pan or not—an inch or two in depth, according to size, of broken flower-pots if you have them, if not, bricks broken to the size of walnuts, or if neither of these be available use small stones or hard coal.   This is what gardeners call drainage.   Then over this place moss, of any kind, sufficient to keep the earth from working down among the drainage.   The reason for this preparation is : if the earth should happen to receive too much water the excess will pass down into this bottom layer and the roots of the plants receive no injury.   For the earth the object must be to have it moderately rich and so porous that it will not bake hard. Good garden soil may do without addition ; if heavy, mix some sand.   Earth from the woods, garden soil, and

9

sand mixed in proportions to make a light, porous soil, will be capital. The plants we shall not try to enumerate. Suffice it to say that any of the plants usually grown in the house in pots will do well in such a box, and each one will have her own preference. If one has no house plants, and can not readily procure them, a box of this kind may be made an object of beauty and interest without expense. Go to the woods and take up sods of moss that have partridge-berry, princes-pine, and such plants, or get cranberry plants from the bogs, or even strawberry plants from the garden. With green moss, such ferns as appear to be evergreen, and low-growing plants from the woods, a fine cheery bit of green may be kept up all winter, only a box filled in this way should not be kept in a very warm room.

STOVES AND STOVE-PIPES.

In the Northern States, at least, whoever takes down the stoves used for warming the rooms before June 10, is sure to regret it. Indeed, our climate is so uncertain, that it is hardly safe to be without the ability to warm at least one room in the house in any month of the year. The taking down of the stoves at the first of May cleaning is a mistake that wise persons do not make more than once. The putting up of stoves in autumn is usually a vexatious business, but much depends upon how the stoves are taken down. It is quite a serious matter for those obliged to attend to it personally, to get, in the fall, the stoves and pipe into a respectable condition for winter use. The following will be found a very easy way of doing a thing that was formerly the occasion of much vexation and trouble. When sheet-iron stoves and pipe are taken down in the spring, first clean all soot and ashes from every part as completely as possible, and have them perfectly dry. Dip a soft cotton or woollen cloth in kerosene oil, and rub over the whole outside surface ; then, with another dry cloth, wipe over the articles again lightly and evenly; then wrap up each piece in newspapers, to keep from dust and air, and store away in a dry place for the season. In the fall, all that they will need to have them look nice, is to rub them over with a dry cloth. All cast-iron stoves are to be treated in the same manner, only add a little dry black-lead or stove-polish to the kerosene oil, and use a small paint-brush with which to apply it. Paint all over outside with the mixture, giving a light even coat, then cover up with newspapers, and set away in a dry place. In the fall, all that the stoves will need is a light polishing with a stiff stove-brush, and, with a little brushing occasionally, they will look nice all winter. Stoves and pipe treated in the above manner will not rust during the summer.

FLOORS AND CARPETS.

There is a strong protest offered, in different ways and from various sources, against our long established practice of making poor floors, with the design of keeping them covered with carpets stretched and fitted to every part, and carefully tacked down. Carpets in daily use cannot be kept clean, except by very frequent shaking and beating, and they do much toward corrupting the air by retaining impure gases, hiding the finest, most penetrating dust in their meshes and underneath them, and by giving off particles of fine wool into the atmosphere, with other dust, as they are swept or walked upon. There is a demand for better floors, not necessarily inlaid or mosaics, of different kinds of precious wood, but made double, of strong seasoned wood, that will not shrink or warp (spruce, however well seasoned, is almost sure to warp), and then carefully finished so as to be durable and easily cleaned. Carpeted floors seem a relief to the house-keeper when once the carpets are procured and fitted to the rooms and tacked down, because they do not show the dirt as the floors do. But oh! when they do get full of dust! And when house-cleaning time comes, and they must be taken up and shaken and whipped, as they well deserve! With warmly-made floors and large warm rugs, couldn't we do without these abominations even in winter? Certainly our rooms would be cooler and sweeter without them in summer. But in that case we must take more pains with our floors, and we must have something better than the common unpainted ones. Oiled floors are better liked than those painted, even for kitchens. Women find that they can oil their floors themselves, and many a kitchen floor has, within a few years, been made comfortable and decent in that way. Boiled linseed oil is used, and two or three coats are put on, one after another, as fast as they are dry. Floors of alternate boards of different kinds of wood are pretty for some rooms, and sometimes a border made in this way, with diagonal stripes, bordered by a straight board on each side, or wood of two kinds laid in checks or diamonds, is very satisfactory. These bordered rooms are especially designed for parlors, or rooms where a heavy bordered carpet or large rich rug is intended to merely cover most of the floor, leaving a margin of about two feet around the edges—a carpet which can often be carried out and shaken free from dust.

Oiled floors do not need hard scrubbing, like unpainted floors, but simply a good washing with warm (not hot) water, often changed. Strong suds of course will gradually remove the oil with which you have carefully filled the pores. Grease spots do not have the same effect as upon an unpainted or unoiled floor, which must be kept free from grease in order to look well, for now it is greased all over ; whatever grease gets on it now, that can not be scraped or wiped up, may be thoroughly rubbed in.

A CHEAP AND NEAT PAPER RACK.

Figure 175 shows a paper rack which is easily made from a pasteboard box, about one foot square and six inches deep. One end of the box proper is cut down along the corner, where it is joined to the sides, and is

Fig. 175.—A CHEAP PAPER RACK.

turned down in line with the bottom. This piece, when the square corners are cut off, in any way that suits the taste, forms the top of the rack, *a*, in the middle of the upper part of which one or more holes are made by which the rack is hung to the wall. The other three sides, *b*, are cut down to about two inches, this depending somewhat upon the size of the box. The cover, *c*, is then fastened to the newly fashioned bottom by a number of ribbons, as shown upon one side in the engraving. Here again the taste may be exercised as regards the size and color of the ribbon, and the number of ties. If preferred, a piece of thin leather, or even strong cloth, can be used to keep the two parts together. The cover and sides may be decorated with small pictures, or in any manner that may be desired. These general directions will allow one to make a useful paper rack, or " catch-all," at a very slight outlay.

KEEP A BOTTLE OF LIME-WATER.

If good milk disagrees with a child or grown person, lime-water, at the rate of three or four tablespoonfuls to the pint, mixed with the milk or taken after it, will usually help digestion and prevent flatulence. Lime-water is a simple antiacid, and is a little tonic. It often counteracts pain from acid fruits, from " wind in the stomach," and from acids produced by eating candies and other sweets ; also " stomach-ache " (indigestion) from over-eating of any kind. A tablespoonful for a child of two years old, to a gill or more for an adult, is an ordinary dose, while considerable more will produce no serious injury. A pint of cold water dissolves less than ten grains of lime, and warm water still less. Pure lime-water, even though pretty closely corked, soon deteriorates by carbonic acid in the air, which unites with the lime and settles as an insoluble carbonate. To have it always ready and good, and at no cost, place into a tall pint or quart glass bottle, of any kind, a gill or so of good lime just slaked with water. Then fill the bottle nearly full of rain or other pure water, and let it stand quietly, corking well. The lime will settle, leaving clear lime-water at the top.

Pour off gently as wanted, adding more water as needed. Some carbonic acid will enter, but the carbonate will settle, often upon the sides of the bottle, and freshly saturated water remain. The lime should be removed and a new supply used once a year or so, unless kept very tightly corked.

A POP-CORN PICTURE FRAME.

A pop-corn frame, so called because that grain was largely used in making it, is shown in figure 176.

Fig. 176.—A POP-CORN PICTURE FRAME.

The back is cut out of thin board, but stiff pasteboard will answer. A row of cherry stones is fastened on both the outer and inner edge of the frame with strong glue. A hazel-nut is put at each scallop; some plum stones are placed here and there, and the remaining space filled with pop-corn of the red variety, all fastened with strong glue. The fruit stones should be well cleaned and the frame will look all the better if these have a coat of varnish before the corn is used, that being sufficiently bright without varnish. Beans of different colors, and other seeds, such as those of the castor oil plant; beech-nuts, chinquapins, very small acorns, and other things will answer for the larger objects, while the pearly rice pop-corn, as well as the little bright yellow variety, will take the place of the red kind. One with a little ingenuity will find no difficulty in producing a pleasing effect. Glue for such uses should be very strong; it is easily made thus : Place in a tin cup some pieces of good cabinet-maker's glue, and pour on enough cold water to well cover them. Set in a cool place over night, or long enough for the pieces to swell up and become limber. Then pour off all the water that will drain away, and set the cup in another dish in which is some water. Set the whole on the stove and allow it to heat gradually. The pieces of glue will dissolve in the water they have taken up; the solution, or made glue will be very strong, and must be kept hot while using by placing the cup in a larger vessel containing hot water. If more water should be needed, it may be added hot and a very little at a time.

SOMETHING ABOUT CARPETS.

A well-made "hit-or-miss" rag carpet is both durable and pretty, and more wholesome to live upon, as it makes less lint than the common wool carpets. Of course we speak of "every-day" or sitting room carpets, not advising "hit-or-miss" for drawing-rooms. It is more work to stripe a rag carpet, and more expensive, and the result is not so harmonious and really tasteful as the even mixture of good rags of various colors in a "hit-or-miss" carpet. These are now quite fashionable. The rags should be evenly cut and sewed with as little bunching as possible.   It saves a deal of time and labor to sew the rags on a machine, but this is more easily done when the rags sewed are all of one color, as in a striped carpet.   To expedite matters in sewing " hit-or-miss " rags, have the rags all cut before beginning to sew.   At least have the general tones of the carpet decided.   Try to have the gay colors distributed somewhat evenly, and the light and dark rags well-balanced through the whole.   Having decided what proportion of each to use (not of each separate color), it is well to parcel them out into a few divisions and then pull rags from each in turn.   For instance, put the black and very dark rags together, the white and light neutral tints (all the medium grays and browns) in one class, including the various small checks. Place all of the gay colors—yellow, red, light-green, and blue—in one division, mixing them up well so that one color will not be all drawn out long before the rest.   It is best not to have too many very gay rags, but to distribute the bright rags in rather short lengths evenly through the whole carpet.

When you sew the rags, have a quantity from each of the four or five grand divisions placed in regular order. Lap the ends and sew straight across with a firm lock-stitch, sew another rag in the same way to the end of one of the rags just sewed, and so on, not cutting or breaking the thread until a long line of rags has been sewed together in one seam.   It is but a moment's work to cut these short seams apart and wind the ball.   Be sure and have good strong warp.

In bedrooms the whole floor should not be carpeted. Short pieces of carpeting, or handsome rugs of suitable sizes, are much to be preferred—one before the bed, one at the bureau, wardrobe, or toilet-table, one at the washstand, and others before easy chairs, desks, or other places especially used for standing or sitting.   These rugs can be shaken out of doors, and the floor can be washed as needed. No kitchen should be completely carpeted, but a few breadths tacked down lightly, so as to be easily and frequently pulled up and shaken, allowing the whole floor to be cleaned, add to the comfort of a much-used kitchen.

BURNS AND SCALDS.

It is in human nature to use remedies for, instead of trying to avoid disease, and we are convinced that pro-miscuous dosing does much more harm than good. Still, however we may object to much dosing, every mother should know what to do for slight attacks of illness, and have at hand a few simple remedies to use in sudden emergencies; and what is of still more consequence, she should know how far she can trust to her own knowledge in a case of illness, and when it is necessary to call in greater skill than her own.

Among the accidents which call for prompt treatment, none are more frequent in the family than burns and scalds, and each mother has her favorite application, which, so far as it tends to exclude the air from the wounded surface without irritating it, is useful. A most effective remedy for burns and scalds, which is simple, and always at hand, is bicarbonate of soda. Sprinkle the injured surface with the common baking soda and cover it with a wet cloth. When the burn is only superficial, the pain is said to cease instantly, and but one application is needed; where the injury extends deeper, longer time and more applications will be required.

BARREL FRAME "EASY CHAIRS."

A large barrel or small hogshead with iron hoops, is cut to the form shown in figure 177, the hoops being first riveted to the staves. Strips or cleats nailed on the inside at any desired hight, support the upper barrel head as a seat. The barrel is mounted on a frame of two

Fig. 177.—THE CHAIR FRAMED.

pieces of wood with casters underneath. A broader, firmer base would be formed of three or four pieces. The supporting brackets are added in front. Figure 178

Fig. 178.—THE CHAIR COMPLETE.

shows how the whole may be upholstered with calico or any other material at small cost. All the above work of "Easy Chair" making may be done at home and involve very little expense.

WHAT TO DO WITH CUTS OR WOUNDS.

Persons who live far from surgical aid, and those who go off on hunting and other excursions, are often at a loss what to do when an accident occurs. In many families, some kind of a liniment or application is kept which is regarded as a universal remedy, but it is often the worst thing that can be applied. In all cases of wounds, recollect that nature makes an immediate attempt to repair damages, and the best thing we can do, is to give her a chance, and aid her.

In the majority of wounds, where no important artery or vein is cut, all that we have to do, is to bring the edges of the wound together and hold them there, and if the wound is not a ragged one, healing will commence at once. Should, however, the edges of the wound be much torn, then use cold-water dressings, until surgical aid can be had ; these may be lint, or any soft cloths, wet in the coldest obtainable water and kept wet over the wound. Should an artery be wounded, the fact will be known by the blood coming out in jerks or spurts, and one must make use of such anatomical knowledge as he may have. Keep cool. If the wound is on a limb, applying a compress somewhere between the wound and the body will stop the bleeding. Tie a handkerchief around the limb, and use a stick to twist it in such a manner as to bring a pressure on the artery. A wounded vein is much less difficult to manage. A bit of lint bound firmly over the wound will usually stop the bleeding. In all such cases, an abundant use of the coldest water is advisable. Perfect quiet is essential ; make the wounded person keep absolutely at rest, and having despatched a messenger for the nearest surgeon, apply cold-water dressing, avoiding the use of all "balsams," "pain-killers," "reliefs," and the like, which are of a highly inflammatory nature, though wounds sometimes get well in spite of them.

CHAPTER VII.

THE LIBRARY.

A HOME-MADE DESK.

Nearly all persons have papers, letters, and other documents, important and otherwise, which they desire to keep and preserve in good condition. They also need a place in some part of the house where letters can be written and other matters jotted down. For this pur-

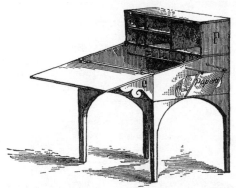

Fig. 179.—A CONVENIENT WRITING DESK.

pose nothing is equal to a good desk, and to be useful it need not be expensive. Any person at all skillful with tools can construct, in two days' time, a desk similar to the one shown in figure 179, and it will answer the purpose quite as well as a desk costing from ten to fifteen dollars. The lid is two feet eight inches long and sixteen inches wide; when open it rests upon supports, *e*, that are hinged to the front of the desk, and fall inward out of the way when not in use. The width of the desk is twenty-eight inches, and two feet eight inches long. The upper portion, at *p*, may be firmly attached to the body of the desk, or left loose as desired; it is one foot high, ten inches wide, with large and small shelves and pigeon-holes. A row of small pigeon-holes is made in the desk, and should be four inches wide, to readily admit an envelope. It is also best to have one or two small drawers, with keys fitted to them, for the better security of important documents. Papers, magazines, and other printed matter may be placed in the open space in the center. A paper holder is also attached to the side, in which unfinished papers and other reading matter may be kept. The lid when open is intended to be used as a place for writing.

ANOTHER HOME-MADE DESK.

This desk, figure 180, is large and roomy, and the writing materials are placed under cover, and are always in

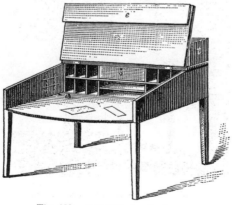

Fig. 180.—ANOTHER WRITING DESK.

their place, ready for instant use. It being so plainly shown, only a few descriptive words will be necessary. A small cover, e, folds over and closes the front of the desk; pigeon holes and a small drawer can be arranged, as shown in the engraving; they may be placed in any other desirable position; the part at *t* could be arranged with shelves, or used as a book-case, or for holding papers and magazines.

A QUAINT, ANTIQUE CHAIR.

Figure 181 gives a design of an antique chair which may be easily made. If the pattern is not exactly reproduced, it will suggest the putting together of a chair

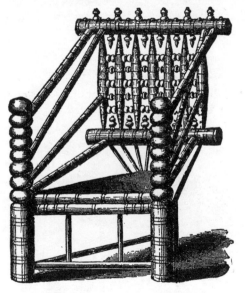

Fig. 181.—AN ANTIQUE CHAIR.

that will be both useful and ornamental, in the farmer's hall, or "front entry," on the piazza, or, if neatly made, even in the parlor. Those who have the use of a lathe can easily turn the parts, or, in the absence of this, such a chair would be pleasing even if made in rustic work, of such material as the red-cedar, or roots and branches of the mountain laurel. The pattern is taken from the President's Chair at Harvard University, Cambridge, Mass. The history of the chair is lost in antiquity, but it has been in use for more than a century, and is still occupied by the President of Harvard when he confers the degrees at the annual commencements of this old University.

A HOOP-POLE CHAIR.

A chair made entirely of hoop-poles is shown in figure 182. The arrangement of the frame is sufficiently shown

Fig. 182.—A HOOP-POLE CHAIR.

in the engraving. It forms an excellent garden chair, much more comfortable than the ordinary rustic one, and can be easily made by any one who can command a supply of smooth hickory saplings. The saplings where they cross one another are fastened by nails. The seat is made of small sticks of the same material, the larger portions of the saplings being used for the legs. Winter is the best time for doing work of this kind, and a chair made in this style costs nothing for materials.

A CUPBOARD AND BOOK-RACK.

Figure 183 shows a cupboard and book-rack that is made from pine matched flooring and is six feet high,

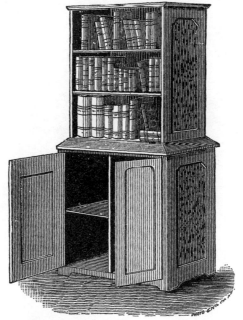

Fig. 183.—A CUPBOARD AND BOOK-RACK.

four feet wide, the cupboard being half the hight. The boards forming the bottom are raised three inches from the ground, giving respectively eighteen inches and fourteen inches clear for the shelves of the cupboard. The shelves of the book-rack are respectively fourteen, eleven, and nine inches from each other. The tongue on the boards at top and on the cupboard is left on, and the top edge rounded, forming a kind of molding. Four boards form the sides of the cupboard, and two the book-rack. This article of furniture can be made of any dimensions desired.

A COMBINED TABLE AND BOOK-RACK.

The table shown in figure 184 is made of butternut, oiled well, and not varnished. Varnished surfaces show every little scratch plainly, and lack the rich appearance

Fig. 184.—TABLE AND BOOK-RACK.

of unvarnished surfaces. Across between the legs are fastened shelves for books ; two on each side. To the legs casters are fixed, thus making it easy to move the stand about the room or to any place where the family gathers. The top is devoted to papers and magazines.

A neighbor has made one out of pine. The legs and shelves are stained to imitate walnut. The top has a covering of pretty cretonne, edged with fringe. Let the boys work at it, and they will soon turn out a most convenient article of furniture, which will be appreciated more and more every day. The children can use it for their school books. Little drawers might be added, like those fastened to the lower side of sewing machine tables, to hold attachments. These could be used for pencils, pens, ink, stationery, etc., thus adding to the usefulness of the table, and making it a sort of portable library and writing desk. About four inches above the center of each shelf a straight piece of wood runs across from leg to leg, forming a support for books put in from each side.

OYSTER-CAN " PIGEON HOLES."

A place for small articles such as letters, valuable papers, seeds, etc., is very important in every house. Such small places of safety are called "pigeon holes," and are

Fig. 185.—A " PIGEON-HOLE " BRACKET.

usually made of thin boards, dovetailed or otherwise fastened together. Figures 185 to 187 show a case of "pigeon holes," which is made of old oyster cans—the square kind—usually found in great numbers about hotels, restaurants, and some dwellings in the interior portions of the country. The cans being thoroughly washed, the end of each is melted out and the edges hammered down and smoothed with a file. Figure 185 shows a bracket shelf with a rack beneath, upon which a number of these cans are placed side by side. The shelf may be arranged for the cans to have the open end in front, so that the contents may be taken out or placed in without moving the can. Some may prefer to have the open end at the top, when each can must be taken out as the contents are wanted. Labels, as " Letters," " Circulars," etc., may be made on the cans as desired. One side of a book-case may be arranged as shown in figure 186.

A thin strip is nailed to the side—the width of the cans from the book-case —and in this space a number of the cans are placed, one over the other, with the open end outward. A case devoted entirely to cans may be made

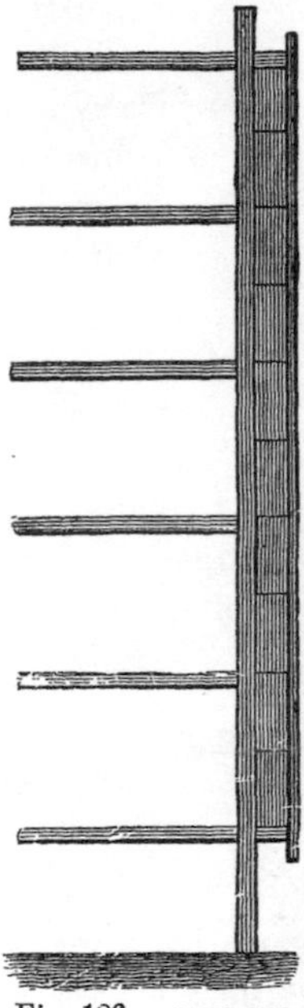

Fig. 186.—CANS BY SIDE OF BOOK-CASE.

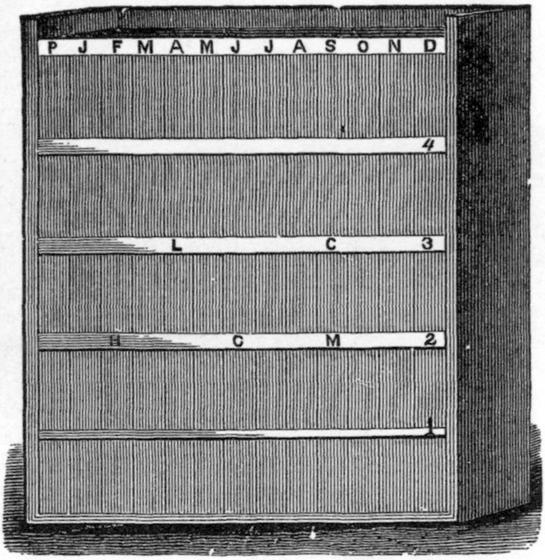

Fig. 187.—A CASE OF OYSTER CANS.

as shown in figure 187. Such a case need not be heavy, and may be set against the wall as a bracket, or placed on the rear of a stand or table. Oyster cans of the square kind arranged in any of the ways here suggested will be found very convenient, and the cheapness should recommend these "pigeon holes" to every one having papers and other small articles to preserve for ready reference.

A CHEAP BOOK-CASE.

Figure 188 shows a form of book-case and desk combined easily made, that will be found of great convenience

Fig. 188.—A CONVENIENT HOME-MADE BOOK-CASE.

to all who can not afford to buy a more costly one. It may be made of pine boards, planed and varnished, or, if desired, stained. A place for writing, and a drawer for keeping the ink, paper, etc., will be a great convenience. A number of drawers could be placed in, if desired, or the case may be left entirely open below the shelf. The main thing is to have a safe place for the books of the household, and a convenient shelf for writing and reading.

A CHAIR FROM A BOX.

The box to make the chair should be three feet square, and when set on end, four feet high. Figure 189 gives a diagram, showing the outlines of the box, and how it is to be cut; the portion from *a* to *b*, should measure

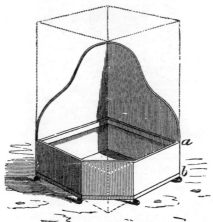

Fig. 189.—DIAGRAM OF CHAIR.

fourteen inches. All the corners should be securely nailed, and cleats placed to hold the seat, which need not be fastened in, as the space below can then be used for the storage of such articles as are not often wanted. Five strong casters, one at each angle, being placed on, the chair is ready for stuffing and covering. It is shown complete at figure 190, where two pieces of carved wood, *c*, are put on as a finish, but to our notion the chair looks better without them. In stuffing such chairs, any coarse fabric will answer; bagging that has been used for packing goods, quite as serviceable as new, may often be had at the stores for a trifle. If green corn-husks be shredded by means of a fork, or some blades set for the pur-

Fig. 190.—THE CHAIR COMPLETE.

pose, into strips as fine as ordinary straw, and dried in the shade, they make a very elastic stuffing. Where there are solid wooden backs, the stuffing can not be knotted, but broad-headed tacks must be driven through into the boards, to hold the stuffing in place. The covering may be such as the purse will allow, or some old dress of suitable material may be turned to account ; for chamber use a covering of chintz will be suitable, but if the chairs are to occupy the living-room, some rep or similar material is preferable. The finish may be improved by the use of heavy cord around the edges, and a fringe or a frill around the seat and bottom.

CHAPTER VIII.

THE SEWING ROOM.

WHEEL-BARROW NEEDLE-BOOK.

The needle-book shown in figure 191 is made of light pasteboard, covered neatly with drab velvet. A small drab-silk wire, wound with the finest of blue chenille cord, is sewed around the bottom, and is bent at the proper intervals to form the handles, legs and support for

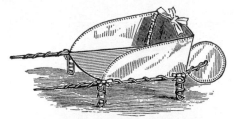

Fig. 191.—A WHEEL-BARROW NEEDLE-BOOK.

the wheel. To the back of the barrow on the inside, are fastened three flannel leaves for needles, red, white, and blue in color. A bow of narrow blue ribbon covers the stitches which secure them, and finishes the places where the legs meet the barrow. A spool of cotton may be deposited in the center, and the whole makes a convenient and ornamental article for the sewing table.

A CONVENIENT WORK-BOX.

Figure 192 shows a neat and desirable work-box that will prove very useful on the sewing table. The box proper is eight inches long, five inches high, and six inches wide. At one side is a small drawer, a, extending across the bottom. The scissors may be secured to

(216)

one end as at *b,* or placed inside as desired. At the right of the handle is a pin-cushion, *e,* while at the left is a little box with lid, *m.* Above and parallel with the drawer, a strip, *p,* is tacked or glued, into which at

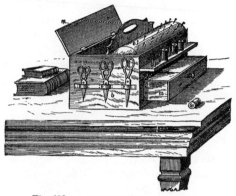

Fig. 192.—A CONVENIENT WORK BOX.

proper interval small pieces of wire are inserted; on these spools may be placed. The box may be made from hard or soft wood, and embellished to suit the maker's fancy.

SMALL ECONOMIES.

It is economy to provide small butter dishes for each individual at table. In this case no butter is wasted by melting on the hot plate, or by mixing with the crumbs or other food upon the plate. Among people who do not put their knives in their mouths, the portions left upon these plates are uninjured, and may still serve as food. Every particle of good butter should be carefully scraped up and saved for shortening, or frying, or for greasing baking pans. Rub corn-meal over very greasy plates, and give it to the chickens. This is a help alike to the chickens and to the dish-washer. Sprinkle salt immediately

10

over any spot where something has boiled over on the
stove, and the place may be more easily cleaned. This
also counteracts the bad odor.

Pins disappear very mysteriously in most families—
very much faster in those where the buttons are not
promptly sewed on when needed. It is certainly wise
economy to take the "stitch in time," and to finish all
garments before they are worn. Plenty of convenient pin-
cushions in a house are a help toward economy. If no
cushion is at hand, a pin picked up is laid down on the
window-sill, or stuck upon the dress—to fall out, perhaps,
into the next batch of bread kneaded. Each child should
be taught to pick up every pin it sees dropped, and to
put it in a proper place.

It is a good plan to have only a few needles of a size
upon the family needle-book, and not to allow children
to help themselves. Do not refuse a needle to a child
who wishes to use it, but keep track of it, and require
it to be returned in good order, and placed where it belongs. Teach the child never to stick the needle upon
the clothing, but, if obliged to lay it down, to place it
upon the work, or upon its needle-book or cushion. A
common, much-used pin-cushion is not a good place for
needles. A leaf of flannel or fine woollen cloth is better.
They are more hopelessly and dangerously lost by sticking
them upon the dress or apron, so that they drop out after awhile, as one goes about.

Careful housekeepers save every scrap of cloth and paper—to sell, if for no other purpose. They use only the
rumpled, soiled papers for kindling fires, and small
scraps even then. The wrappers that come on magazines
and papers are saved for scribbling, for ciphering, or for
wrappers again when turned the other side out. Put the
clean wrappings of dry goods bundles away for use.

A rag-bag is a necessity, hung by a strong strap in
some convenient place, and a few smaller, and possibly

ornamental, scrap-bags in other parts of the house, help toward economy. Every sewing machine needs one. Do not place into the rag-bag good, strong patches, though small, such as you will need for patching clothing, or may use for stocking heels or mitten patches. These should have a separate place. All long strips and pieces suitable, should go in with the carpet rags. The tiniest scraps of woollen cloth are valuable for rugs. Every bit of silk or velvet should be saved by itself. Some one may be glad to make a silk bed-quilt or sofa-cushions of them, and they often prove great treasures for button-covers or for making fancy articles.

A SIMPLE WORK-BOX.

Figure 193 shows a work-box that is ten inches high, eight inches wide, and six inches deep. The drawers

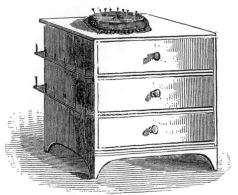

Fig. 193.—A CHEAP AND CONVENIENT SEWING BOX.

are two inches deep inside, and are made of one-quarter-inch material; the rest is of one-half-inch boards. Each drawer has a brass knob. The top projects three-quarters of an inch all around. Two strips, with wires for spools are placed on one side, the other end has a strip of leather tacked on for scissors. A pin-cushion is placed on the top. The cost of everything besides labor was twenty cents.

A COMPACT QUILTING FRAME.

The frame is supported by two standards or end pieces, one of which is shown in figure 194. The upper horizontal portion is thirty inches long, and of two by three-

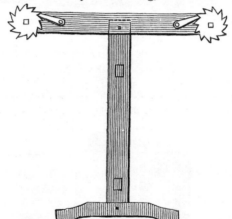

Fig. 194.—STANDARD OF QUILTING FRAME.

inch stuff; between this and the foot is an upright thirty inches high, with two mortises for the slats. There are two slats, seven feet long and one by three inches; each end is cut to form a tenon, which passes far enough through the upright in figure 194 to allow of a three-eighth-inch pin; when the slats are in place, and the pins driven in, the whole is very firm, and may be moved about if desired; the lower slat answers as a foot-rest for those working at the quilt. The two rollers, figure 195, may be round or eight-sided, seven feet long and two

inches through ; one end has a round bearing, an inch
and a quarter in diameter ; the other end has a similar
bearing, and beyond that it is an inch square, to hold the
ratchet-wheel shown in figure 194.   The ratchet-wheels

Fig. 195.—ROLLER TO HOLD QUILT.

may be of hard-wood, four inches in diameter and an inch
thick.   A strip of cloth is tacked to each roller.   The
advantage of this frame over most others is the small
space it occupies, whether in use or not.

A HOME-MADE WORK-TABLE AND BASKET.

Home-made furniture, if well put together, will be
quite as serviceable as that purchased from the cabinet-
maker and upholsterer, and may be made at a cost quite
insignificant as compared with the other.   In the matter
of appearance, there is a cosy home-like look about these
home-made articles that is much more in keeping with
the surroundings of those in moderate circumstances,
than any showily upholstered work of the shops.   A
barrel, and a few pieces of lumber, will furnish the materials for the frame-work of a table.   The heads of the
barrel answer for the base and the cover ; these being in
two or three pieces, are fastened together by two strips
nailed on in the manner of cleats.   To the center of one
of these fasten an upright standard of a convenient hight,
as in figure 196 ; this may be done by putting several
strong nails through the base, and it would add greatly
to its strength to place two or four short braces between
the base and the standard ; these are not shown in the
engraving.   The strongest and best hoop of the barrel is
selected, and four braces, of staves split in halves, or
other material, are attached at half way up the standard,

one end of each being firmly nailed to the standard, and
the other end to the hoop.   The frame being finished, as
in figure 196, it is to be covered with such material as
may be desired, or may be at hand.   Glazed cambric of
some bright color, covered with Swiss muslin, laid on in
plaits, makes a very pretty covering; but the matter of
covering is one that admits of a wide variety, and most
house-keepers will be inclined to utilize some material at

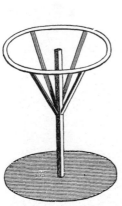

Fig. 196.—FRAME OF TABLE.   Fig. 197.—TABLE COMPLETE.

hand.   The covering should be fastened with small tacks,
and left full enough to allow of its being gathered in at
the middle, by means of a cord or band, as in figure 197.
The second barrel-head is to be covered on both sides
with the material, and may be fastened by a hinge to one
of the braces, or left loose.   A ruffle or a plaited strip
should be placed around the cover, and around the top
and bottom, to hide the edges of the covering material,
and give a finish to the whole.   If the covering is not sewed together, but the edges merely lapped over where they
meet, the lower part of the table may be used to hold

slippers or other articles, which may be placed in through the opening thus left.

AN ECONOMICAL TABLE COVER.

By the following method a simple, cheap, and yet very pretty cover for a table or stand may be quickly made. A heavy double-faced canton flannel is now manufactured, in a variety of colors, having the nap on both sides, and it is on sale generally. Either this or the single-faced can be used, but the double-faced is preferable

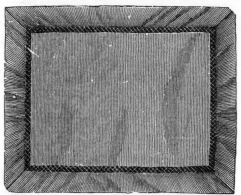

Fig. 198.—A CHEAP AND PRETTY TABLE COVER.

on account of its extra thickness. The shade can be selected to match the furniture. When cut to a suitable size, it is bordered with a contrasting shade of the same material of any desired width. But this is best made of the single nap flannel, as the double would be a little clumsy. The border is cut of double width and folded so as to leave the fold for the outside edge, and stitched on. To cover the seam, sew on a strip of velvet or velveteen with cross or feather-stitch of filoncelle, of contrasting shade; gold is preferable. This comes in all colors and costs but little, and each thread can be split into two or three threads. The finished mat is shown in figure 198, made from a photograph.

A NEAT CATCH-ALL.

This little catch-all is to be hung in a sitting room or bedroom, to hold the little trimmings and scraps of waste paper, which make such an untidy litter if left around loose. The rings are crocheted from wrapping cord, and the bag is made of blue or red cashmere. For the rings, first make four chain stitches, join, and over these make fifteen stitches in double crochet (see figure 199.) Each ring is made separately, and when fifteen

Fig. 199.—ONE OF THE "RINGS."

are finished, they are sewed together with strong thread, in the shape shown in figure 200. A similar half diamond is made for the other side. Cut of pasteboard two pieces, the size of the rings after being sewed together, and cover each on both sides with cashmere. To these pieces sew a puff four inches wide, and long enough to allow for gathering. A piece of the cashmere, five inches wide, is sewed around the top. The upper edge is turned down to make a hem an inch deep. A second row of

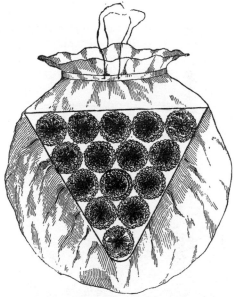

Fig. 200.—THE CATCH-ALL COMPLETE.

stitching is put an eighth of an inch above the first, to make a casing in which is run a colored cord for a draw string. The bag is hung up by the cord which is knotted together, and the knot drawn into the casing.

A GOURD SCRAP-BASKET.

Large sugar-trough gourds can be made into a number of pretty and useful articles, among which is the scrap-basket, shown in the illustration. To make such a basket select the largest gourd possible, cut off the top, remove the seeds, and scrape and sand-paper the inside surface until it is perfectly smooth. Cut down the smaller piece to the proper size, and glue it to the lower part of the larger one, which forms the basket. The gourds are often a little irregular in shape, and the best decoration for them is a pattern similar to the one given, which is an imitation of the designs on the earthen jars made by the Indians of New Mexico and Arizona. The pattern is put on with common paint and a small brush. It may first

Fig. 201.—A GOURD SCRAP BASKET.

be traced with a pencil. Red, black, or dark-brown paint should be used, or the pattern may be done in two colors, black and red, or brown and red. The baskets will be very useful for a variety of purposes, but are particularly intended for setting by the table, to hold papers and magazines, or to receive waste papers and scraps. The gourds can also be made into very pretty work-baskets by providing them with a lining. From the smaller sizes, handsome covers for flower pots can be made, painted in some pretty patterns, ornamented with scrapbook pictures, or in any other tasteful manner.

A DOLL PANEL.

The face, and perhaps figure, are cut from one of the infinite variety of scrap pictures, and pasted on. Then the puppet is dressed in a real costume; tiny little lace cap, or beaver hat, while skirt, silk dress, cloth sack,

Fig. 202.—A CARD OR PANEL DOLL.

even a collar round her neck, and wee bits of slippers, or shoes, made from an old kid glove, on her feet. All is as complete as the outfit of any mother's darling on

Broadway, excepting only that her clothes are fastened
with mucilage, instead of being sewed and buttoned. It
requires very skillful fingers to make these panels nicely,
but when finished, they are a charming remembrance for
the children for New Year's and birthdays.

A DUCK PEN-WIPER.

A neat and attractive wiper for pens may be made as
shown in figure 203. A young duck, that has died soon
after hatching, is stuffed and placed in a "nest" made
of a series of cloths. The edges of the pieces, to serve

Fig. 203.—DUCK PEN-WIPER.

as the wiper, may be cut with pleasing outlines. We do
not advocate the hatching of young ducks for making
pen-wipers, but as accidents often befall young fowls,
nearly every farmer's poultry yard will furnish subjects to
be used as here described. A young chick, though not
so pretty, will answer well in place of a duckling.

A CARPET RAG LOOPER.

The looper, shown in figure 204, is made out of an old
saw blade, and is about four inches long, and three-
quarter inch wide in its widest part. There should be a
slot large enough to admit the ends of the rags. In use,

force one end into a block of wood, then push a rag down
over the looper, push another rag over on the opposite

Fig. 204.—A CARPET RAG LOOPER.

side, and place the loose end of the first rag through the
slot and pull both rags from the looper. Rags may be
looped quickly with this instrument.

SCRAP-BOX OTTOMAN.

To make the convenient article shown in figure 205,
select a strong wooden box, and fasten on a lid with
small hinges. Around the sides of the box place a curtain of some pretty material; chintz, or furniture calico
is suitable. Tack it closely to the upper edge of the
box, and put a few tacks around the lower edge to hold
the cloth in place (figure 205). Lay several thicknesses of

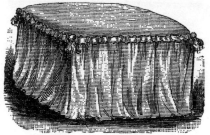

Fig. 205.—A SRAP-BOX OTTOMAN.

old carpet, or worn out comfortables on the top of the
lid, and tack on a cover of chintz. Make a full frill of
the chintz about three inches deep. Tack this around
the edge of the lid, so that it will hang over the top of
the chintz upon the sides, and tack a heavy worsted tas-
sel to each corner of the lid. It is, however, the interior

arrangement of the box that makes it of greatest use in
every sewing room.   On one side is tacked three pockets
(figure 206,) of some strong material.   The pockets on
the opposite side are as wide, but only half as deep,

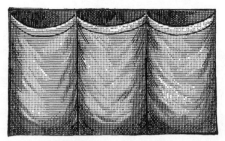

Fig. 206.—END OF OTTOMAN.

making six on that side.   On each end are two deep
pockets, similar to those on the side.   These pockets are
for holding scraps of goods used in working, thread,
braid, buttons, and anything which is needed in general
family working.   On the lid are tacked two strips of

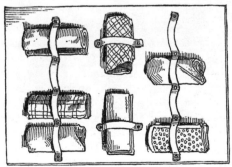

Fig. 207.—UNDERSIDE OF THE LID.

inch-wide elastic ribbon (figure 207), divided into several
loops, with two loops across the space between the longer
strips.   These are to hold rolls of muslin, or any goods,
or patterns which it is more convenient to keep by

themselves. The space left in the middle of the box gives a place for more rolls of scraps, or for holding articles for sewing.

A HANGING CARD-BASKET.

So long as invitation, wedding, calling, and other cards are used, card-receivers of some kind will be employed, and new designs will be appreciated. Card-baskets are

expected to be not only useful, but ornamental as well, and in most cases they are made more to fulfil the latter than the former purpose. The basket shown in figure 208 is an imitation of a balloon, and is intended to be suspended from a side hook, like those used for hanging bird-cages, and may be hung from a gas-fixture. It is largely ornamental, and allows of a great variety in its construction, and a display of taste in its ornamentation. The basket shown in the engraving is eighteen inches long, from the attachment to the bottom of the basket, the "balloon" being eight inches across. It is constructed of white

FIG. 208.—A BALLOON BASKET. Bristol-board and heavy woollen yarn. The balloon is six-sided, the parts being fastened together by narrow ribbon, which is glued to the joined edges. The basket is made of the same material, and in the same manner. The basket is suspended from the balloon by six portions of the wollen yarn, the balls being of the same material. The sides of the balloon, and those of the basket, are decorated with pictures or flowers, to suit the taste of the maker. When neatly done, this basket is very pleasing, and well serves its purpose.

A NEAT PATTERN OF TATTING.

If it were not for tatting, many a garment would go without ornamentation; many an hour would be spent in idleness, and it may be that some mouths would go with-

Fig. 209.—A DESIGN FOR TATTING.

out food. The art of tatting has progressed so rapidly that the designs which may now be wrought out of ordinary thread by a little shuttle in skillful hands, is quite surprising. In figure 209 a pattern is shown which combines the elements of simplicity and beauty, and is of such a form as to be easily built out, or enlarged upon, in all directions. The pattern is the single wheel and its attachments. When made in a single row it is used for

the edging of garments. If constructed in squares of
four wheels—as in the engraving—or nine, sixteen, etc.,
it makes a tasteful end for a necktie. When the square
is larger and made with coarse thread, a fine and delicate
tidy for a chair or sofa is produced.

A GOOD SCRAP BAG.

For small rolls of stuff, a scrap bag with pockets, in
which scraps of lace, silk, embroidery, etc., etc., can be
kept by themselves, is a very useful and convenient
article. It is made of oil-printed calico, with a gray
ground, and pink roses, and green leaves in a vine over
it. One yard is sufficient for a bag. Cut two pieces of
the cloth, each fourteen inches
wide, and eighteen inches long.
For the pockets cut four pieces,
each five inches wide, and five and
a-half inches deep, rounded slightly at the bottom. Make a hem
nearly an inch deep across the top
of each pocket ; stitch it twice to
make a casing into which run an
elastic cord, making a long knot in
each end to keep it from slipping
back. Gather the pockets a little
at the bottom; turn in the edge all
around, and stitch them on the bag.

Fig. 210.—A SCRAP BAG.

After the pockets are on, sew up the sides of the bag,
and the bottom also, so that the four points will meet.
Hem the top of the bag to make a frill one inch-and-a-
half deep ; stitch it twice, and run a cord in the casing
made by doubling and twisting zephyr, "Germantown"
or "Berlin" wool. Small tassels made of wool the color
of the cord may be put on each corner and on the bottom.

A CARD BASKET.

A pattern for a card-basket of perforated card-board, with a hexagonal base and six five-sided pieces around the sides is shown in figure 211.   Let each side of the

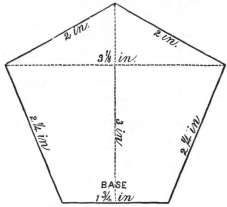

Fig. 211.—PATTERN FOR CARD-BASKET.

hexagon be exactly one inch and three-quarters wide. Cut the side-pieces of the shape of figure 212.   Bind the pieces around, with narrow lute-string ribbon.   You can

Fig. 212.—ONE SIDE OF BASKET.

either work some little design on each piece with silk or worsted, or fasten a little picture upon each.   Overhand the pieces together and be careful to sew to the hexagonal base the side of the five-sided piece which measures an inch and three-quarters. A little bow of lute-string at the top (inside) of each side seam, will add to the effect.

EASILY MADE INSERTIONS.

We have selected four kinds from among the many patterns, and show them of actual size. Insertion being the

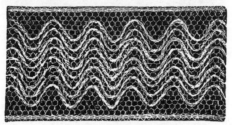

Fig. 213.—WAVE INSERTION.

accepted name for an ornamental fabric, sewed between the portions of a garment, its use will be understood. The ground-work of these insertions is cotton mosquito lace, which may be obtained at the dry goods stores of any size or mesh to suit the taste. The size shown in the engravings, is perhaps the most convenient to work upon. The thread used in these is the double and single

Fig. 214.—A LOOP PLAN.

" A " brand. Figure 213 is a graceful waved design, made by passing the needle—which should be a large one —through the meshes of the lace, in a curved line.

Figures 214 and 216, are made with larger thread. In figure 215, a diagonal loop is formed, making a vine-like figure, with a central stem. Much more elaborate de-

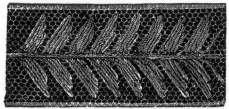

Fig. 215.—A VINE FORM.

signs are made—in fact, the limit to this work depends only upon the patience and ingenuity of the designer.

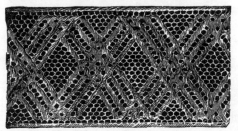

Fig. 216.—DIAGONAL DESIGN.

Those here given, are of the more simple kinds, easily and rapidly made, look neat, and are durable.

CATCH-ALL.

To make this catch-all, cover a piece of tin or paste-board, twenty inches long, and four wide, joined into a ring, with bright-flowered chintz. To the lower part of the ring run a strip of material twelve inches deep, and a yard long, seamed together. After it is sewed on, gather it at the bottom to make a full, fluffy bag, and add two small tassels of zephyr. Around the upper edge sew another piece of material, like the bag, six

Fig. 217.—A CATCH-ALL.

inches deep, and long enough to go around the ring easily. Sew a ribbon or braid an inch and a half from

the upper edge to make a casing, in which run a narrow
silk braid, or a cord, for a draw-string.   Fasten a heavy
worsted cord at each side, by which to hang it up.

SATCHEL FOR SCHOOL BOOKS.

It often happens that children have to walk quite a

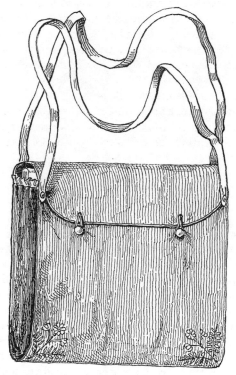

Fig. 218.—A SATCHEL FOR SCHOOLBOOKS.

distance to school, and they should be provided with a
satchel for carrying books and luncheon.   It should be

large enough to hold an atlas, and have long straps for
suspending it over the shoulder. To make one, cut a
piece of heavy linen, or Burlap canvas, twenty-four
inches long, and fourteen wide, two pieces fourteen
inches long, and four wide, and one fourteen inches long,
and eight wide. Double the largest piece in the middle,
and sew the two pieces in at the sides, as shown in figure
218. They should be fulled in at the bottom and a
strong rubber cord run in a casing, to draw them at the
top. Sew the other piece to the back, after the front
has been rounded and bound with braid. Sew two buttons on the front, and two loops on the flap as fastenings.
The straps are made of strips two inches wide, doubled,
and stitched together, and fastened to the satchel with
buttons. The seams may all be made on the right side,
and bound with red braid, but if put on the wrong side,
they should be over-cast, for the satchel does not need
lining. A pattern in red wool may be worked in each
lower corner.

INEXPENSIVE HOME-MADE MATS.

A firm, durable mat, of any size desired, more or less
ornamental, and quite inexpensive, may be made as follows : In a capacious bag placed out of sight in a closet,
deposit all good remnants from the family sewing, bits
of gay colored flannels, cashmeres, pieces of old woollen
coats, pants, etc. From time to time, when too weary
for other work, and the eyes are too tired to read, cut
these materials into strips, as for rag carpet, and sew
them together, and wind in balls. When enough material
has accumulated, with large wooden needles, such as are
used for knitting shawls, knit these rag strips back and
forth into mats of any desired length and width. A
variety of effects can be produced by sewing together and

winding on separate balls the strips of the same color and knitting them in color bands; or they may be so thoroughly mixed as to give a mottled surface. If the cutting and sewing be done somewhat evenly, the surface of the knitted mat will be quite smooth, and the mat itself firm and lasting. It can be finished with a border of home-made fringe; or with a strip of two shades of

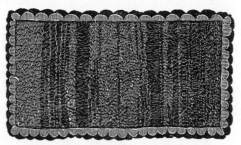

Fig. 219.—A HOME-MADE FLOOR MAT.

cloth cut into scallops, one strip extending a little beyond the other, as seen in figure 219, made from a photograph of a mat fifteen by thirty-two inches. A variety of these mats may be used in front of wash-stands, commodes, and other exposed places.